USING FIVES FOR WRITING

Mary Shea & Nancy Roberts

D1036529

LEARNING SCIENCES INTERNATIONAL

1400 Centrepark Blvd., Ste. 1000
West Palm Beach, FL 33401
717.845.6300
email: pub@learningsciences.com
learningsciences.com

Printed in the United States of America

22   21   20   19   18   1   2   3   4   5

Publisher's Cataloging-in-Publication Data
provided by Five Rainbows Cataloging Services

Names: Shea, Mary, author. | Roberts, Nancy, author.
Title: Using FIVES for writing : communicating, thinking, and
    learning effectively / Mary Shea [and] Nancy Roberts.
Description: West Palm Beach, FL : Learning Sciences, 2018.
Identifiers: LCCN 2018941748 | ISBN 978-1-943920-30-3 (pbk.) |
    ISBN 978-1-943920-32-7 (ebook)
Subjects: LCSH: Composition (Language arts)--Study and teaching.
    | Literacy--Study and teaching. | Effective teaching. | Education-
    -Standards. | Learning, Psychology of. | BISAC: EDUCATION /
    Teaching Methods & Materials / Language Arts. | EDUCATION /
    Professional Development. | EDUCATION / Standards.
Classification: LCC P53.27 .S54 2018 (print) | LCC P53.27 (ebook) |
    DDC 808.042--dc23.

This book is dedicated to all young authors. Working with them inspires and informs best practices for writing instruction as well as teachers' understanding of each writer's uniqueness.

—Mary Shea

Writing opens a voice to many who haven't been heard. It is the communication that is so needed to share, express, and show. I dedicate this book to those students who have welcomed me in as a part of this journey, from pen to purpose.

—Nancy Roberts

Acknowledgments

As teachers—as individuals—we know that we stand on the shoulders of those who support us in the moment or through the legacy of ideas and information others have published. The total of our pedagogical knowledge is built from multiple sources of information, countless experiences trying to make that knowing operational, refinement of practice in meeting the needs of students, and learning from the work samples (informal and formal) that students construct daily. It's an ongoing, never-ending process of *becoming*—becoming better and better at what we do. It takes a community to develop a teacher's expertise—the researchers and authors we read to learn seminal and current concepts, the colleagues we work with who demonstrate and share their talents, the parents who help us understand their children, and the students who work actively with us in a teaching-learning dance that allows everyone in the classroom to reverse roles naturally and seamlessly.

We extend appreciation to Andrew Shea (high school English teacher), Sarah Kozarowicz (middle school literacy teacher), and their students for sharing teaching ideas and processes they've used successfully along with student compositions constructed by writers in their classrooms.

The editors and staff at Learning Sciences International, particularly Dana Lake, have generously provided advice for revisions and edits throughout the process of composing this book. This insight, graciously offered, has helped us shape what we wanted to say efficiently and effectively.

—Mary Shea

From the early days of looking for a better tool for students to develop success in writing, I have never been alone! Students and fellow teachers have shared their concerns and ideas on the task of writing. First, we worked in giving it a purpose, answering the *why* we were writing in each step we needed to fulfill when completing a meaningful finished product. Creating writing lessons that worked for all students and provided a path to success was the goal. With the support of many, the development of the ABBC writing format/process has evolved into the text before you.

It is with gratitude that I acknowledge the hours of conversation and discussion shared with Sarah Kozarowicz, coworker and friend, in reviewing and digging deeper into the needs of students at each grade level in various content areas. In addition, the patient and reflective input of Diane Scrooger, who shared and collaborated regarding writing with the younger students in our care, has been consistent. Lastly, I want to thank both Lynn Murphy and Dawn Hammand, Literacy Learning Center assistants, for their attention to the details of writing and to the students in front of them.

Learning Sciences International editors and staff have offered sound advice and direction in this text. They additionally provided insight and encouragement in our bringing forward this writing strategy—one that's aligned with the FIVES reading strategy—to our fellow educators and their students.

—Nancy Roberts

Table of Contents

Introduction

Reading and writing are more appropriately conceived as running in parallel and utilizing many of the same basic mechanisms.

—Stephen Kucer

This book functions as an expansion of *the FIVES strategy for reading comprehension* (Shea & Roberts, 2016a), which focuses on leading students to internalize a mental model for applying tools for reading with understanding through the self-production of prompts as guides. Each letter represents a skill to be applied for grasping concepts, information, and vocabulary in texts. They also relate to personal connection-building (that is, with background knowledge and experiences), elaborating, expanding, and the ability to express conclusions succinctly and accurately.

F represents *facts*. Before readers move to higher-level thinking, they need to acquire facts with which to work; these become the grist for digging deeper into ideas and thoughts. *I* is associated with *inferences*. Readers read between the lines, putting what's in the text content (tc) with what's in their minds (background knowledge—bk; and experience—e) to construct an inference. Thus, I = tc + (bk + e) (Shea, 2012). It's important to remember and respect that life's circumstances and opportunities, friends, family, culture, and school have shaped the background knowledge and experiences that students bring to a text (Shea & Roberts, 2016a, 2016b); this explains the variance revealed across readers' inferences with any text read. *V* is for *vocabulary*. "Words are important; they have power" (Shea, 2011, p. 194). To make their intent clear, authors try to use precise words. Some of these may be unfamiliar to readers who need to fully understand words, terminology, and expressions used to comprehend; informational texts are often replete with more sophisticated, topic-specific words, making attention to vocabulary particularly essential. *E* represents *experiences*. Readers evaluate, expand, elaborate, and make connections based on personal experiences (that is, from background knowledge and life). This conglomeration is woven into the meaning constructed with texts read. *S* is for *summary*. Shea (2012) states, "In a summary, the reader rephrases the gist of the text with a modicum of inference—or none at all" (p. 77). Readers reveal the accuracy, extent, and depth of their comprehension, ability to distinguish main ideas and significant details, and degree of clarity in expressing what they've gathered from the text in their summary. Summarizing becomes an ongoing metacognitive behavior; as they navigate through complex text, readers form brief mental summaries (Shea & Roberts, 2016a, 2016b). The FIVES strategy links the receptive language process (that is, reading) with expressive language processes (that is, speaking and writing). This book focuses on that link of reading (gathering ideas) to expression of thinking and conclusions drawn—particularly in written form.

The FIVES strategy for reading comprehension calls for expression of thinking at each point. Students identify (that is, orally and in writing) facts found, inferences made, vocabulary meanings, and experiences as the basis for their expansions and elaborations; they share their oral or written summaries with peers. Students' practice with FIVES leads to the internalization of a process—a mental habit—for navigating through text, gathering ideas, processing them, thinking deeply, making personal connections, expanding and elaborating on information gleaned, forming and explaining conclusions, organizing content, and expressing thoughts.

The ability to express thinking clearly as well as provide logical rationale for it is a fundamental life skill as well as an academic one that can become a *gatekeeper*. The inclusion of reading and writing tasks on formal and informal tests becomes a factor related to students' ability to demonstrate their learning and achievement. "That's how writing has become a gatekeeper for student promotion and graduation, as well as for schools' annual yearly progress [AYP] and federal funding" (Cole, 2007, p. 31). This text recognizes reading and writing as *parallel processes* that need to be simultaneously a focus at each level of English language arts (ELA) instruction (Shea, 2011). Kucer (1985) called reading and writing *parallel processes* in discussing research findings in education, cognitive psychology, and linguistics that examined the underlying thinking in "acts of comprehending [reading] and composing [writing]" (p. 317). Thus, *Using FIVES for Writing: Communicating, Thinking, and Learning Effectively* naturally blends with instruction on the FIVES strategy for reading comprehension.

In this book, the *FIVES* acronym for reading comprehension is adapted to the cognitive processes involved with composing text.

> *F* poses that writing is a *Fundamental life skill*
>
> *I* reminds writers to *Identify the core request*
>
> *V* directs writers to *Visualize the plan*
>
> *E* encourages *Expanding the process to an essay*
>
> *S* describes *Synthesizing information from multiple sources*

The chapters that follow take readers through the steps for integrated instruction of FIVES for both reading with understanding and writing with confidence and clarity. Beyond the emergent level, writers start with a well-constructed, focused paragraph: the ABBC.

The plan for the ABBC paragraph came to Nancy and her colleagues as a need when they realized how many secondary students were asking, "Where do I begin?" Some students easily move from reading (that is, the intake of information) to the parallel process of writing (the expression of what they've learned with clarity and fluency), but many others struggle at some level or with some aspect. In today's technological society of text shorthand and minimal responses, instruction and practice with academic writing and other types of extended compositions become even more of a challenge (as well as a necessity) for academic writing, career-related messaging, and success in life. The process and craft of composing full messages must be carefully and developmentally taught and included in curricular designs across grades. Redirecting blame for writing weakness with "They should have been taught this in *x* grade!" is not only inappropriate, it's not useful. At every grade, instruction must address all the literacy processes as they relate to the curriculum for ELA and content areas. Post-instruction activity that follows includes teacher modeling, collaborative work, and independent work—that is, reading and writing to, with, and by students—the *I do*, *we do*, and *you do* (Fisher & Frey, 2007). Always, there is a gradual release of responsibility to the learner as scaffolds are faded; but all fading is done differently to meet students' needs.

The ABBC format for constructed responses (CRs) is a process that helps writers write with purpose and process. It is about communicating understanding, persuading readers of your premise, or sharing information. Being able to compose succinct, coherent print messages is essential today more than ever, when both schools and careers expect much to be done concisely, clearly, and in print rather than verbally.

With the ABBC format, students are taught to *Announce* their purpose for the writing. Then, they need to *Build up* and *Back up* the premise in their lead with evidence (for example, information in the text) with, minimally, two points; the writer also lets readers know the source of claims or statements, using citations. Finally, CR writers *Connect back and Conclude* the response or answer. The ABBC format is also a process for preparing public or formal speeches that share information or attempt to persuade. The structure helps students consider how they will respond to what they've read, heard, and watched—information they've assimilated and processed. Readers also learn to evaluate information, statements, or claims (that is, ones heard or read) before accepting them as valid. This is an essential life practice, whether considering advertisements or ideological arguments.

Teaching in Steps

Determined to provide students with a writing plan that could be used successfully across all subjects, Nancy reviewed several suggestions in professional literature with colleagues. After considering each, synthesizing the information, and distilling the elements deemed to be a good fit for their situation, the consensus was the ABBC format for the constructed response—an acronym that would be easy to remember (that is, *It's as simple as ABC!*) and represents essential components for a complete, focused, constructed response that would be successful in any domain of knowledge. Nancy's familiarity with teachers and students in the district, acquired in her role as a literacy specialist in elementary and secondary classrooms, informed her as she led the implementation of the ABBC format. It became a writing strategy that all teachers could incorporate; it created a common language that was used in instruction and understood by students—and there would be developmental performance expectations (that is, benchmarks) across grades. Anchor charts posted in the classroom serve as constant reminders of the format. Students glance at them while planning, writing, and self-assessing their CR before submitting work. When instruction in the writing process starts early—with an approach and expectations that are consistent across grades—and continues through secondary levels, confusions created by classroom-specific approaches and differences in the language of instruction used are lessened. See figures I.1 and I.2 that are from elementary classrooms.

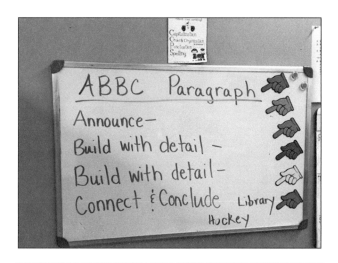

Figure I.1: ABBC steps.

Figure I.2: ABBC steps with example sentence.

CHAPTER 1

(F) Fundamental Life Skill

*I am always doing that which I cannot do, in order that
I may learn how to do it.*

—Pablo Picasso

Meeting School Standards

The NAEP (National Assessment of Educational Progress) test, administered across the United States to random samples of students in specific grade levels, requires students to write a constructed response paragraph that is supported with evidence from texts provided. *Constructed responses* (CRs) are paragraphs in which students integrate their comprehension of information gathered from sources with language skills to express learning related to the question or prompt they were given. Perceived as a real world competency, CR writing has been increasingly used in standards-driven assessment tasks (Tankersley, 2007; Shea, Murray, & Wright, 2015). Sometimes called *open-response* items, CR prompts allow multiple avenues for correctly answering a question or petition. Students construct personal meaning with the information they've read; they are also expected to convincingly provide evidence (that is, rationale) for ideas from the text, background knowledge, and/or experience. Calkins (1994) calls this *grounding*; the writer explains the grounds on which the answer is based. It appears that many students are woefully unprepared for success with these tasks; curricular reform that promotes targeted attention to authentic writing instruction and practice has been glacial in speed.

In a past test administration, 70 percent of all fourth-, eighth-, and twelfth-grade students were identified as writing below basic levels; they clearly failed to meet

NAEP standards (Graham & Perin, 2007; Persky, Daane, & Jin, 2002). Data from the 2006 SAT showed the largest drop in scores in thirty-one years, though adjustment to the exam's new writing section is a confounding factor (Cole, 2007). Limited attainment of writing competency starts early and persists; alarmingly, Salahu-Din, Persky, and Miller (2008) reported that 66 percent of fourth graders fell below the cutoff level on the NAEP. Ramifications extend beyond the writing measured on any test; difficulty learning across content areas and grades usually correlates with difficulty in reading and writing texts in that domain, acting as a gatekeeper for success (Graham & Perin, 2007; National Commission on Writing, 2004; Shea, Murray, & Wright, 2015).

The U.S. Common Core State Standards (CCSS), adopted by forty-two states at one point, outline expected outcome competencies in writing (CCSSO & NGA, 2010), appreciating that "reform of writing instruction is [remains] a necessity in this country, as almost two out of every three youngsters do not write well enough to meet grade level demands" (Graham, Hebert, & Harris, 2011, p. 2). Analyses of formal assessment data from students' writing performances reflect that inadequately logical, unpersuasive arguments (Ferretti, MacArthur, & Dowdy, 2000) occur frequently in students' expository writing (Harris & Graham, 1999). Although writers' workshops have flourished for a period and continue to be found in classrooms, a preponderance of writing in that community has been personal choice narratives; there's a notable scarcity of interdisciplinary writing instruction and extended tasks in subject area classes (Applebee & Langer, 2006; Gilbert & Graham, 2010). Too often, content area teachers feel that such integrated ELA instruction takes attention away from content and curricular demands. Actually, it can become synergistic with both when it's done well (Pytash & Ciecierski, 1995).

Increasingly, the effectiveness of writing instruction in classrooms is essential for ensuring that students meet the standards for writing competence (Gilbert & Graham, 2010) and can use writing to learn. Without creating a balance with increased instruction in exposition writing—that's specific to domains of knowledge—and guided student practice, improvement will be difficult to realize.

Breaking Down Broad Goals

National standards focus on broad, meaningful applications of skills that are literacy related and domain specific, recognizing the role of language in learning across all subject areas. School faculty design curricular objectives to meet the broadly stated standards, appreciating the needs of their students, cultural context of the community, and resources (that is, material and personnel) available. Preparing students for college and career readiness is essentially more about teaching how to create and use knowledge to reason, innovate, communicate, learn, collaborate, adapt, and be flexible than it is about ensuring mastery of facts and isolated skills (Shea & Roberts, 2016a, 2016b). Goals for writing emphasize *using* writing to think, learn, and communicate; steps in learning how to write effectively are valued for their application effect. There's parallel learning of writing with reading as students demonstrate their thinking, knowing, and learning—incorporating an array of sources (Shea & Roberts, 2016a). They

- compose clear, coherent, and organized writing focused on the task, purpose, and audience;
- conduct short research projects that build knowledge through investigation;
- draw evidence from texts to support responses; and
- use technology and digital tools to research information, compose, publish, and collaborate with others. (CCSSO & NGA, 2010)

CCSS further delineate a balance of students' purposes for writing (National Assessment Governing Board, 2007).

When composing in any genre—for any purpose, the writer must

- think about the topic;
- gather his ideas;
- review the ideas;
- plan what he wants to say;
- decide how the telling will be organized;
- construct the text;
- revisit and refine the presentation; and
- determine if, how, when, and where he wants to share his message. (Shea, 2011)

Standardized state assessments increasingly include expectations that students are competent with CR writing and can use it to demonstrate what they have learned in subject areas. This presents urgency for identifying "powerful instructional techniques for teaching writing that are effective with good, average, and struggling writers" (Graham & Harris, 2005, p. 32). Since many students have been identified as unprepared to write beyond the personal response (Purcell-Gates, Duke, & Martineau, 2007), CCSS has defined a guide for ensuring balance in the percent of students' engagement with different functions for writing.

Table 1.1: Purposes for Writing

Grade	To persuade	To explain	To convey meaning
4	30%	35%	35%
8	35%	35%	30%
12	40%	40%	20%

Source: National Assessment Governing Board, 2007.

Writing as a Life Skill

Writing acceptably "can be described as a culturally mediated function" (Luria, 1998, p. 16) with prescribed, but malleable, forms that one must follow carefully to be considered literate. Although an unfair assumption, writing that's replete with errors is too often correlated with lower intellectual ability and/or social status. Being literate leads to opportunities such as those related to learning and achievement, career, and one's level in society; lack of it restrains them.

Content and procedural knowledge, communication facility, problem-solving ability, and interactional competency are skills associated with successful people. Each requires a developed capacity to apply literacy processes fluidly across all topics, contexts, and texts. The inclusion of literacy tasks on content area tests is intended to emulate how people are expected to acquire and apply knowledge in the world (Shea & Roberts, 2016a).

Lack of writing success marginalizes and limits students in school and in life. They become disempowered—held up by the *gatekeepers* (Cole, 2007). Writing well has become just as essential for academic success as it is for success in the world. Low-level literacy skills become a hurdle that's increasingly difficult to overcome (Shea & Roberts, 2016a, 2016b). Those who have learned to communicate what they know, feel, and believe in writing that is clear, cohesive, substantive, and persuasive often apply the thought and planning processes required for such composition to other tasks, including solving problems in their lives (Hudson, Miller, & Butler, 2006).

Literacy processes (that is, speaking and listening, reading and writing, viewing and visually representing) are symbiotic, growing simultaneously when integrated in use. Each receptive form (that is, listening, reading, and viewing) reinforces the expressive form (that is, speaking, writing, and visually representing) (Shea, 2011).

"Writing can contribute to building almost every kind of inner control of literacy learning that is needed by the successful reader" (Clay, 2001, p. 12).

Learning to Write Is a Process

Shaughnessy (1977) challenged the use of terms such as *incapable, indifferent*, or *disadvantaged* for low-functioning writers even when they performed as strangers to academic tasks. Instead, she suggested that they wrote as *beginning writers*—with intentionality and little that is random or illogical. Although older, these writers are actually at the emergent stage of writing development. For any number of reasons, their writing history is sorely lacking. Like beginners, they must learn from instruction at the point of current development, have time for abundant scaffolded practice, and receive targeted, sensitive feedback at the moment of need. Studying their writing history, what skills they use effectively, what they try to use but confuse, and the background knowledge they possess are appropriate places to start instruction that brings positive responsiveness (Luria, 1998). That instruction must also address the full range of writing tasks.

With their preponderance of assign-and-assess writing tasks, school curricula appear to assume that, once students can write sentences, journal entries, or personal narratives, they transfer that knowledge to any genre. The absence of a sequenced, developmental approach to teaching academic writing provides evidence to support such a conclusion. Some teachers have included writing tasks in content area lessons (Kipper & Duggan, 2006; McDermott, 2010), but too often these have been incidental short-answer responses (Gere, 1985) infrequently preceded by explicit instruction or modeling of what is expected or how to effectively plan and execute such tasks. More extended expository writing, if done at all, is limitedly required in school; such writing is often assumed to be too difficult for students to do and too difficult to evaluate (Shea, Murray, & Wright, 2015). Vacca, Vacca, Gove, Burkey, Lenhardt, and McKeon (2009) suggest that struggling writers—ones particularly disengaged with academic writing—feel apprehensive about being successful with a task they're unprepared to accomplish. This makes them understandably unmotivated to try. They would rather appear unwilling than unable. When required to write, they plan haphazardly, generate a minimum of continuous text, and present thoughts in a stream of consciousness that reflects a disconnected repetition of ideas from sources—anything to produce a quantity of print that camouflages shortcomings. The result is writing that lacks clarity, cohesion, focus, personal voice, and direction (Christenson, 2002).

Phinney (1988) found that struggling students disengage academically when they meet difficulty unless they're offered *discrete* support—specifically, strategies that help them make sense of content to be learned and how to apply it in assigned tasks. All learners, but especially those who struggle with the composition process, need explicit, differentiated, and developmentally appropriate instruction in the knowledge and strategies associated with successful writing; they also need ample time for supported writing practice that meaningfully integrates these aspects with content across the curriculum (Mason, Harris, & Graham, 2002). Writing competence is likely to grow with instruction that fulfills those criteria; the success that follows increases students' self-efficacy and motivation for writing (Graham, Harris, & Troia, 1998) and learning. Starting where students are developmentally in writing, teaching and scaffolding forward become essential.

Students are more likely to persist when they can envision success through effort. Research reports that effective disciplinary literacy instruction (that is, focused on the specificity of literacy skills related to the discipline) also has a generative effect; it is associated with a positive impact on students' learning in the domain (Lesley & Matthews, 2009; Misulis, 2009). Such "writing helps students think about content, reflect on their knowledge of the content, and share their thoughts" (Fischer, Frey, & Williams, 2002, p. 72). In content areas, writing to learn often centers around inquiry. Graham and Perin (2007) note that "inquiry involves a series of activities where students collect, analyze, and apply data to complete a specific writing task" (p. 31). Through well-crafted prompts, teachers stimulate students' use of a myriad of higher-level thinking processes, rereading of text, and meaningful discussion as preparation for writing-to-learn domain-specific content (Parsons & Ward, 2011; Streitwieser, Light, & Pazos, 2010). A well-designed scope and sequence of writing instruction and curricular objectives—sensitive to the diversity of students' needs in any setting—are more likely to ensure that developmentally appropriate, differentiated writing instruction and content learning hold a rightful place in ELA instruction. Knowing what needs to be done is only the first step; the road to the destination needs to be built and maintained.

Teaching How to Write Is Also a Process

Historically, many educators held that students must acquire basic reading skills before they can learn to write or spell. Curriculum for early childhood—right from the start and onward—reflects this stance; writing had a back seat to other language processes. Regrettably, this belief goes against evidence we have of young children's understanding of and engagement with the function and forms of writing as a communicative act yet is accepted by many teachers. It leads students at any level to suppress their drive to write in forms that are developmentally appropriate yet unconventional (Clay, 2001). It could—and should—be otherwise.

Right from the start, when we teach students how to read, we read *to* and *with* them—and we allow them to read independently and with peers (Mooney, 1990). Introducing the reading process with the full act of reading presents the function of the process first and foremost—and it allows students to experience the full benefits of reading that satisfy curiosity, inform, touch the heart, help one understand others and the world, and so much more. Learners become motivated to persist at learning how to be proficient readers. With the function fully revealed, we gradually introduce the forms of the reading process to emergent readers at a point where they can appreciate how knowledge of these forms will enable them to join the *reading club* (Smith, 1988).

From primary years, we teach students distinct pieces of the reading process while always continuing with the reading of continuous texts in all genres about all kinds of topics of interest. We teach the sounds, the letters, and how the letter-sound relationships are used to create words; we show combinations of letters, patterns of letters, and words in English that do not follow phonetic generalizations. Then, we go further with how the words are combined to create sentences and sense in delivering a message. There are numerous separate objectives in the developmental scope and sequence for reading instruction across the grades, but the overall goal is that students use their knowledge of language forms, genre structures, and grammar to read for meaning, information, and pleasure—to successfully use literacy skills to navigate their world and communicate with others in and out of school.

So, then, why do classrooms not offer this same developmental process of immersion, demonstration, and scaffolded practice in writing? Effective teachers write *to* and *with* students daily; they also ensure that there is ample writing *by* students every day. One learns to read by reading—and learns to write by writing. Teachers need to repeatedly show students that, even for experienced writers, "the right words and sentences just do not come pouring out like ticker tape most of the time … the first draft is the child's draft, where you let it all pour out and then let it romp all over the place, knowing that no one is going to see it [or evaluate it] and that you can shape it later" (Lamott, 1994, p. 22).

Too often, young children are introduced to the reading processes and, then, expected to automatically be able to write. Writing tasks are assigned and assessed in classrooms, but explicit prewriting instruction appears scant. We know that reading and writing are parallel processes—growth in one supports growth in the other; they should be taught and used simultaneously and authentically from the beginning. Young children don't discriminate in using the processes intentionally before they come to school (Shea, 2011). Like reading, effective writing instruction—from the beginning and forward through the grades—responds to what students are trying to do—where they are on the journey of learning the forms of language that allow functional writing for personal messaging.

Writers gradually, through instruction and observation of use in anchor texts (that is, books used as models of writers' craft), learn the grammar and conventions expected for writing with clarity (for example, where to use capital letters and punctuation, proper use of verb tense, sentence structures, and more). As developmentally appropriate, teachers show writers how to add spark and interest to messages with descriptors—such as adjectives and adverbs that *paint a picture* for readers. Demonstrations are given that model the addition of details, evidence, clarification, and mood—all intended to inform, persuade, or evoke emotion. Yet we find that when attempting to put what they've learned into practice, some students feel overwhelmed. They stare at the blank page (or computer screen); they simply don't know where to begin writing, how to organize it, and how to conclude their message.

Young students are logical thinkers in their explorations and constructions when writing; they notice print around them and attempt to perform the observed writing behaviors of significant others in their world. Ranges of appropriate achievement and spurts of growth are very common at each stage of learning development; both are highly influenced by intellectual ability, physiological factors, interest, motivation, and culture, as well as the quality and quantity of experiences students have in and out of school (Caine & Caine, 1997; Jensen, 2001; Rushton, 2001). Students' approximations need to be accepted and respected (Cambourne, 1999); they form the basis for targeted instruction at the point of need (Shea, 2011). Explicit instruction, abundant modeling, and scaffolded practice with genuine, sensitive feedback is needed along the way, as described. But along with that, a clear, concise, and concrete plan to get writing started in any genre provides the courage to *get off the ground*. Creative, artistic venturing—writing over the genre *lines*—comes gradually, once writers feel comfortable and confident with the task. Until then, writers need to start with a basic plan—just as someone learning any other craft starts with a simple task and pattern to complete it.

Researchers have identified stages in writing; these make sense of the range of student performances while recognizing that students will often demonstrate skills out of expected sequence or across multiple stages. "Development is a process not [merely] a series of stages nor a set of sequentially learned skills" (Dyson, 2003, p. 11). Stages offer a guide to an individualized developmental process rather than a rule; they provide a lens for identifying where students are and what they need in the moment instructionally to review, reinforce, or move forward in a risk-free, comfortable, and supportive setting (Newman, 1984, 2004).

Upper-elementary and secondary students are typically somewhere in the *transitional* stage of writing and spelling (Schickedanz, 1999). Some are closer to the beginning of that stage, while others are approaching conventional grade-level expectations. The transitional stage is actually lifelong in many ways. The literate person continuously perfects the use of language skills for more refined and sophisticated applications and acquires new ones that meet current demands of language performance and agility. Purpose and need drive continuous language growth in life and careers.

Working persistently on writing filled with voice—writing that communicates personal understandings, expresses feelings, or attempts to convince others—flows when students are invested in the process and when they have a passion and purpose for what they want to say and a degree of choice in how to say it (Shea, 2011). In an effective writing classroom, students talk about their work; they listen and respond to text written by others. Along with writing and reading, they're speaking and listening. These expressive and receptive language processes are used as they are in the world—interactively. That's when growth in one fosters growth in the others—when they become synergistic (Shea, 2011).

Pause and Ponder

With colleagues, reflect on and discuss the following prompts.

1. What are the basic writing skills that any person needs to be successful in school and an effective communicator in life?

2. Discuss where and how the standards align with levels of writing proficiency that one needs for academic achievement and success in life.

3. How do the classrooms in your school (or classrooms you have observed) teach writing in ways that help students reach the standards?

CHAPTER 2

(I) Identify Prewriting Considerations

Tell me and I forget. Teach me and I remember. Involve me and I learn.

—Benjamin Franklin

Examining the Prompt: Questions and Petitions

Prompts posed as *questions* typically start with interrogative pronouns (for example, who, whom, which, what), how, when, or why and end with a question mark. They request answers from the recipient—answers that provide information or explanations of thinking. Another type of prompt is *petitions*. Petition prompts establish directives using words like list, describe, outline, report, or explain; each specifies expected behavior for the response—from reporting information to expressing a rationale (Cole, 2009; Shea & Roberts, 2016a, 2016b).

Posing strong prompts defines a purpose as well as a guide for reading. Questions or petitions that teachers present become models for considerations readers eventually ask themselves before, during, and after reading. There needs to be a balance between the types of prompts that direct the acquisition of information and the application of it in higher-order thinking. "Questions lead readers deeper into a piece" of text (Zimmerman & Hutchins, 2003, p. 73). Effective prompts stimulate inquiry; they promote intense engagement, propelling a quest for knowledge. Not all prompts inspire the same depth of thinking, nor are they meant to. Prompts can be thick or thin. They lead readers to content at the surface (that is, what's stated) and that which requires deeper digging and thinking (for example, inferring, connecting). *Thin* prompts center on statements found in the text—in a single sentence or across several sentences or paragraphs; *thick* prompts require thinking between and beyond the lines of text—analyzing the information stated as well as what is implied (McLaughlin & Allen, 2000; Tierney & Readence, 2000; Shea & Roberts, 2016a). Thin and thick prompts stimulate the various levels of reading behavior described in Bloom's taxonomy of thinking levels (Anderson, Krathwohl, Airasian, Cruikshank, Mayer, Pintrich, Raths, & Wittrock, 2001). At the Teaching Channel website (https://www.teachingchannel.org/videos/structuring-questioning-in-classroom), a teacher discusses the art of questioning. Transcripts of the lesson can be downloaded. The more complex the thinking, the thicker the prompt that stimulated it. The responder must learn to analyze prompts carefully; understanding what is asked or expected is the first step toward a successful response.

Unsuccessful responders often fail to attend to the specifics of the petition prompt and/or consider the specific behavior requested. The result is a response that is limited and/or misdirected. Teachers need to explicitly teach how to analyze a prompt, clarifying the distinction between question and petition prompts, noting that questions require answers and petitions expect responses in a specified format. Instruction should include a focus on how to analyze what is requested and build a plan for completing the task. Effective teachers model written expression that has depth and clarity—that reflects the writer's understanding and thinking (Shea & Roberts, 2016a).

Constructed responses typically define a prompt (question or petition) very specifically, making what is requested clear. Students who have had the experience of constructing prompts when reading (that is, in FIVES, Shea & Roberts, 2016a) are better prepared to understand how prompts are constructed and consider what a successful answer or response must include. *The FIVES Strategy for Reading Comprehension* (Shea & Roberts, 2016a) outlines meaningful experiences that involve students in constructing prompts followed by detailed responses or answers. When writers go off track in their answer or response, it's often because they misread the prompt, went down a tangentially related aspect of the issue, or don't have the information required for accuracy and completeness. Essays can simply be longer answers or responses to a given prompt. At other times, the author defines the prompt for the essay to be written—an aspect of a larger issue or topic on which he wishes to do research or express personal conclusions or opinions. Crafting the effective prompt for an integrated response essay (IRE)—calling for an essay-length composition—is a challenge. Writers often fall into the trap of trying to cover too much in a single piece of writing (Phenix, 1990).

Narrow the Focus: Identify Issue, Problem, Question

When constructing an effective question or petition prompt for a CR or IRE for which a thorough and thoughtful answer or response can be accomplished in the expected format, the prompt must be targeted on a narrowed and specific aspect of an issue or topic. That can be difficult at first. Student authors of prompts—especially for an essay or research paper—often have a prompt that would take a full text to address completely. Or the prompt is too vague, allowing the answer or response to meander or wander into unintended areas or information that appears to have no or only slight relevance.

Efficient and insightful answers or responses to well-defined prompts build a body of knowledge and thinking; the many different analyses of aspects of an issue become puzzle pieces that link to a whole. Appreciating such a role for each prompt, there is less of an inclination to pose wide-ranging ones. Narrowed and targeted prompts can still, however, be open ended, inviting differences in reasoning and conclusions based on the source(s) referenced and individual background knowledge integrated as rationale. Some examples of prompts for CRs or IREs are as follows.

Examples of Well-Written Prompts

CR: Read the article "A Lifeline for Lions." Does the title accurately describe the importance of what is explained in the article? Explain your reasons.

CR: Read the article "The Fosbury Flop." How did the Fosbury Flop change the sport of high-jumping? Use information in the article to support your answer.

CR: Erosion along its banks causes a constant movement of sediment in a river from upstream to downstream. Explain how this sediment affects a river.

IRE: Winters were hard in the New World, and the colonists had to think of clever ways to fight the cold. Describe ways in which colonists fought the cold to survive the winter.

IRE: Describe how a large decrease in the algae population would impact a water ecosystem. Include immediate and long-term effects.

IRE: What factors influenced the U.S. government's hesitancy to enter World War II in the early years of the conflict?

These *constructed response* prompts call for a focused paragraph response reflecting students' knowledge and thinking. The IRE prompts call for an *extended constructed response*—an *integrated response essay* that has additional evidence as well as expanded explanations for each and a more developed introduction and conclusion section.

Function and Forms in Language Processes

Models of clear oral presentations and well-crafted writing in all genres can be used as *anchor texts* (that is, models to be examined for their attention to design, format, and message clarity). In her book *Wondrous Words*, Katie Wood Ray (1999) describes just how to do this and suggests anchor texts to use for each facet of writing craft. Students are guided to examine how authors accomplished their communicative purpose through their competent use of language and presentation qualities (that is, the language processes successfully fulfilled their intended *function*). Digging deeper into the content of model communications, *forms* (for example, genre structure, word use, transitions) that enabled the efficient execution of the author's function are identified, defined, and analyzed. Appreciating the importance of function and understanding how forms ensure that communicators are successful are essential for developing competent speakers and writers who can construct short or longer messages.

Components of an Effective Response

This section describes the basic requirements for an effective response—addressing the prompt, staying on topic, paraphrasing, and using strong vocabulary and transition words. These five factors are essential to writing competency and need to be integrated into the ABBC framework.

When, How, Why

Assessments—whether classroom based or formal ones—that include *constructed responses* (CRs) attempt to measure students' ability to recall, organize, and infer from information in a source and use that to construct an effective expression of what they've learned and the thinking they've done in a coherent, cohesive, and concise paragraph. When thick prompts (that is, questions or petitions) are posed, more than one word is required in the answer or response. Such prompts differ from binary choice ones or those where a one-word response is sufficient (for example, "Did you lock the door?" or "Is there milk in the fridge?"). In the everyday world as well as in academic settings, responses with rationale are often expected—ones that demonstrate responsiveness to instruction, learning, thinking, and competence in summarizing, explaining, persuading, instructing, and more. Single-word or short responses assess recall or memorization; they have a place and purpose, but they do not reveal how well or thoroughly the learner has engaged and interacted with information to absorb it, personalize it, make connections with it, synthesize it with prior knowledge, evaluate it, and demonstrate deep comprehension of the content from a source. Successfully constructed response paragraphs require reporting of information from the source, inferences made, and conclusions drawn when thinking about the content. They also expect meaningful integration of a learner's prior schema on the topic—prior knowledge that has been cross-referenced with the new information to determine compatibility or need for verification. Personal prior knowledge may be lacking or have dated or incorrect information; information in a new source may also be questionable. Readers must resolve such cognitive dissonance through an evaluating, revising, and deleting process based on verification of evidence from all sources; this lessens the possibility that constructed responses are infected by incorrect schema or shallow readings that lead to writing with limitations in content accuracy.

This process of applying higher-level thinking to knowledge absorbed from a source and examining it with prior knowledge on the topic for possible connections provides a rich tapestry for writing; the weaving process expands initial understanding gained from reading. "Writing is one of the most powerful tools for developing comprehension because it can actively involve the reader in constructing a set of meanings that are useful to the individual reader" (Irwin, 1991, p. 24). After reading, the reader should have learned something, confirmed something known, acquired additional schema on a topic, or experienced an emotional response—all of which become grist for expressing understanding and personal meaning either orally or in writing. Such expressions from young children are typically spontaneous and automatic, but they can also be thoughtful and rehearsed. With effective demonstrations, guided practice, and sensitive feedback, children learn the social expectations for sharing ideas.

Adults who are significant in students' lives (for example, parents, teachers, others) provide them with strategies, processes, and skills that enable them to develop as communicators who can define and defend their ideas. The artful teacher engages students in expressive language processes (for example, conversation, writing, and visually representing) focused on applying these in parallel with receptive ones (for example, listening, reading, or viewing) to realize, to evaluate, to organize, to integrate, to assimilate, and to connect with what was learned in personal ways (Shea, 2011). "Effective teachers know that students who are forced to converge on predetermined inferences, conclusions, connections, or themes are not engaging in higher-level thinking" (Shea & Roberts, 2016a, p. 103). Past primary grades, demonstrations of learning progressively demand more sophisticated products—more details, more evidence, more higher-level thinking. Students who have not been given the opportunity to develop the balance of shifting across all language processes fluidly, using them strategically and interactively to come to knowing and to show their knowing, are disadvantaged, but not disabled. With targeted, mindful intervention, gates can be opened.

It is up to the teacher to disallow gatekeeping that results more from limitations in teaching than lack of ability. Daily, across subjects, there must be some amount of authentic reading and writing *to*, *with*, and *by* students (Mooney, 1990). Assuring this inclusion in the curriculum (that is, across disciplines) is likely to result in expected developmental achievement in each language process, acquisition of content knowledge, and competence in applying language and literacy to continue learning across increasingly more complex domains of knowledge (that is, *disciplinary literacy*).

When students ask questions about tasks assigned for the *reading and writing by students* (Mooney, 1990) component, they quite often want an answer to when, how, and/or why. Typical ones might include "When do we have to get this reading done?," "How do we start the writing?," "Ms. Roberts, why do we have to write about that now?," or some combination of all three. Students are naturally looking for details that will help them meet the challenge; the teacher's responsibility is to provide complete directions and answers to such queries. She points out that writers need to be as accountable for details in completing the task assigned as they wish the teacher to be in clarifying the directions; responsibility is reciprocal.

The teacher explains the qualities of an efficient, detailed, and complete answer or response to a prompt based on content students have read, heard, or experienced. Nancy uses an example from her own childhood to demonstrate the importance of *the rest of the story* for students. She shares how one day she came home in fifth grade and told her parents, "Our physical education teacher was mean." Her parents didn't get riled by the claim, but her father asked Nancy to explain *why* she concluded that he was mean. She answered, "He doesn't like me and three other kids in my class." Again, her father wanted more of an answer, more information to back up what she was saying—*evidence* to support the charge. Her father asked *how* she knew he didn't like them. This time Nancy got more to the point. "He wrapped me and the others, who asked to have the windows closed, up in the team aprons because we were cold and had us sit to the side during gym." Finally, her dad asked *when* this happened. Her father told her to start wearing long sleeves on gym days. He also spoke to the teacher, and no one was ever wrapped warm again. After sharing the memory, Nancy asks students the following questions:

- Why is it important to include *why*, *how*, and *when*, when trying to convince others of an opinion?

- What other question words should be considered in answering a prompt?

- What guide words would help you formulate a detailed, clear, and complete answer or response?

The class discussion of their reactions and comments typically reflects their evolving realization on responding successfully to prompts. They realize how they need to be attentive and actively engaged when listening and reading to be more prepared to think about content and apply ideas as discussants or writers (Gipe, 2014). Goodlad (2004) suggests that students receive approximately 70 percent of new information through the aural mode, making attentiveness and engagement essential for learning. Through such instruction and facilitated discussion, students begin to understand how to approach the tasks requiring the expression of knowledge and thinking; they appreciate the purpose for each step as well as the payoff for completing each brilliantly.

The acronym *ABBC* offers a plan; the teacher explains what each letter stands for as an essential component for a successful constructed response. Examples are provided for class discussion; students are invited to collaboratively construct question and petition prompts along with their answers or responses. She introduces the ABBC process and *shows* students—through explicit instruction, modeling, and practice, practice, and more guided practice, along with genuine feedback sensitively delivered—the tools and strategies that enable them to effectively use expressive language processes for academic purposes. That knowledge and the realization that others expect they can do it is empowering. It fuels grit, perseverance to get it right, and success.

Addressing the Prompt: Effective Leads

The opening volley in any good piece of writing grabs the reader's attention and draws him into the composition, making the need to know what comes next compelling. To accomplish that, the writer *never gives away his thunder*—or tells all in the opening. Rather, with a well-placed pinch of mystery, writers spur readers on—to whisper to themselves, "Tell me more" (Cole, 2009). Creating an effective lead is a craft that can be developed. It starts simply. A good lead introduces the reader to the author's intent and helps the writer stay on topic.

Writers are taught how to turn *question* prompts into effective leads. Rephrasing the question as a statement is a place to start. Each ellipsis in the following examples represents points where more information from the source would be added during the modeling.

> **QP:** What was the most prominent cause of the Industrial Revolution? Explain.
>
> **Lead—A:** Although many causes are described, one could be considered to have had more influence than the others as a cause for the Industrial Revolution. It appears to have propelled the changes that affected everyone in some way. **B:** First, ... can be traced through all the economic, financial, and social conditions of the time; this created .... **B:** As additional evidence, ... **C:** That's why .... could be considered as the most prominent cause of the Industrial Revolution.

Students could also be called to respond to *petition* prompts to demonstrate their knowledge on the same topic. Both types of prompts are used by teachers as well as formal assessments. Students need to know how to create a good lead for either that directs their response to be focused and targeted on the prompt.

> **PP:** Identify what could be considered the prominent cause of the Industrial Revolution. Explain.
>
> **Lead—A:** The Industrial Revolution evolved because of the economic, financial, and social conditions of the period, but one factor appears to have propelled the changes that affected everyone in some way. **B:** First, ... can be traced through all the changes of the time; this created .... **B:** As additional evidence, ... **C:** That's why .... could be considered as the most prominent cause of the Industrial Revolution.

Effective writing teachers elaborate on instructional steps for teaching the process of creating effective leads for constructed responses. This step is foundational; a strong constructed response will be guided by a good lead that sets a direct path for the writer to follow that doesn't stray from the destination or purpose.

Staying on Topic: Narrowed and Focused

Writers begin slowly to build basic leads using the prompt as described to craft an opening that grabs readers. Growth in writing is a developmental process that requires lots of instruction and modeling followed by many starts, retries, and adjustments. Learning to write an effective lead will seem daunting at first, but students gradually begin to understand *how* it is doable. That skill needs sufficient time to be nurtured; it is key to all that follows. Competence with the Announce step makes remaining steps easier to accomplish successfully.

A strong lead has that hint of mystery that begs for more details that follow as explanation or evidence; it creates a clearly defined highway for both the writer and reader to follow. The effective lead identifies the boundaries of that highway and what needs to be met along the route to ensure that the reader's query—*tell me more*—was answered before a conclusion was offered. When the route was followed as suggested in the lead, the writer can confidently conclude, "That's why …" or "These reasons explain why …"

It's important to expect and respect early attempts at constructed responses that fulfill the requirements but may not be masterpieces of literary craft. Understanding the framework of the genre and crafting answers and responses that demonstrate acquired knowledge of curricular content, thinking, and developmentally appropriate writing competence come first. Refinement of one's writing craft and the infusion of creativity and personality will be added more easily to a strong foundation.

After the lead, the writer adds evidence that fulfills the direction of the answer or response suggested at the opening. In the constructed response (CR), each point of rationale—each B—has a sentence or more of explanation based on the source mingled with the writer's background knowledge and experience; in the integrated response essay (IRE), each step of the A, Triple B, C comprises a paragraph or page to fully develop the author's premise. Thinking in each step of the CR and IRE is clearly stated, reasoned, and on point. The writer doesn't stray off topic or offer peripheral details. A simple statement (developed to a paragraph or page in the IRE)—one that ties together the B points made and connects back to the lead—provides a conclusion. As students become adept at writing CR paragraphs and IREs, they begin to add *spice* or *punch* to their conclusions. However, start at the intersection of simple and straightforward for both CRs and IREs.

Paraphrasing with Voice

Right from the start, it's essential to ensure that students understand how words or ideas can be plagiarized. Quoting the words of others is only done to emphasize a point; another author's exact words are used sparingly. Ideas formed and information gathered are paraphrased thoroughly; that requires writers to restructure sentences, restating content in a personal voice.

Writing *voice* is difficult to describe but often recognized as one does a familiar speaking voice. When you read voice in text, it reveals something about the author. Tompkins (2010) defines voice as a writer's personal style; it is "what breathes life into a piece of writing" (p. 62). Culham (2003) colorfully describes voice as "the writer's music coming out through the words" (p. 102). Writing characterized as having voice reveals the author's style, humor, and sensitivities through the choice of words, phrases, figures of speech, and/or ways of expressing ideas. Effective paraphrasing with voice is challenging, time-consuming, and glacial in its development toward competency (Gunning, 2010). How to paraphrase must be modeled, modeled, and modeled by the teacher using different genres and contexts; it must also be practiced, practiced, and practiced by developing writers who continuously receive supportive feedback. Collaborative class paraphrasing that follows teacher modeling builds students' competence and confidence with the task.

Cole (2006) suggests allowing students to work in small groups (for example, in threes or fours). Assign a reader, a reteller, and a scribe to each *Paraphrasing Pod* (Cole, 2006). Give each pod (small group) one copy of the text. One student is assigned to read the text aloud while the others listen. The text is set aside. The group talks about what was read. The reteller orally summarizes the information. The group discusses this summary, refining and revising; together they construct an oral summary, which the scribe records. The students review their summary to further revise and edit it as needed. Roles and pods change to do the next summary. This practice prepares students to individually restate information gathered in their words; they appreciate why they need to do it as well as how to do it.

Students can move to working in pairs—in a *pair-share* (Cohen & Cowen, 2011). Partners read the same passage and set it aside; they summarize it individually in their words. Then, partners review their summaries collaboratively, comparing and critiquing each. Rotate the partners, allowing students exposure to and discussions on differences of interpretations. Along with discussing the content of what was read and differences in interpretations, students are guided to consider the vocabulary from the passage they've used as well as strong words of their own they've included in their summary, which add clarity, sophistication, style, and power to the message.

Using Powerful Words

Bintz (2011) describes a person's working vocabulary as the total of words known and used by the individual for communication; this includes words used when speaking and writing (that is, in expressive language) and words understood when listening and reading (that is, receptive language). The sum increases across developmental stages as does the expectation for depth and breadth of words selected in a literacy context.

Words have the power to evoke emotion, interest, curiosity, deeper understanding, and clarity of intent. Word choice is a craft commonly evaluated in assessing writers' work at all levels (Culham, 2003). We expect students to use increasingly more sophisticated and precise words in their writing and speaking as well as domain-specific words when relating information in a content area. Words that have been thoroughly introduced, discussed, and used in context are more likely to find their way into students' writing as well as into their conversations.

Extensive research has demonstrated that more new words are learned by students through reading and listening attentively during enriching experiences than through instruction; there simply isn't enough time to teach all the words that high-functioning students have amassed in their repertoire of known and used words (Cunningham & Stanovich, 2001; Jenkins, Stein, & Wysocki, 1984). Students with rich vocabularies notice words read and heard; they have a curiosity about words. They make associations with the context in which the words were met as well as their background knowledge and experience; they analyze the word fully (that is, using context clues, structural components), consider multiple meanings and nuances (that is, subtle distinctions) implied by the use of the word, and incorporate the word into their conversation and writing appropriately (Beck, McKeown, & Kucan, 2002; Kindle, 2009; Scott, 1993).

Connecting Sentences and Paragraphs with Transition Words

For smooth connections between sentences in the CR and from the introduction to the first paragraph of the IRE's body of content, students need to learn how to use transition words to draw readers smoothly from sentence to sentence and paragraph to paragraph. A printable version of transition words for classroom anchor charts can be obtained at http://writing2.richmond.edu/writing/wweb/trans1.html (Taraba, 2015). Draw students' attention to these words in texts read, and model how to use them when doing a TA/WA (think aloud / write aloud) modeling or collaborative writing; post them prominently in the classroom as a reminder of appropriate choices. See figure 2.1. Transition words are signals of what is coming just like road signs on a highway. Words such as *First*, *Next*, *Then*, and *Finally* anchor the reader in the sequence of the author's telling. As well as announcing a step, transition words or a sentence at the end of a step can create a bridge for readers to the next step in the CR or IRE. A sentence sequence such as "Along with this reason, another should also be considered. Next …" draws the reader from the first *B* to the second in a CR—or IRE.

Showing Relationships within and between Sentences

Transitional words and phrases connect and relate ideas, sentences, and paragraphs. They assist in the logical flow of ideas as they signal the relationship between sentences and paragraphs. In prose, the material is supported and conditioned not only by the ordering of the material (its position) but by connectives which signal order, relationship, and movement.

Some of the more commonly used connectives are listed below. Note especially how these **connections function to develop, relate, connect, and move ideas**.

1. **To signal _addition_ of ideas**	and, also, besides, further, furthermore, too, moreover, in addition, then, of equal importance, equally important, another
2. **To signal _time_**	next, afterward, finally, later, last, lastly, at last, now, subsequently, then, when, soon, thereafter, after a short time, the next week (month, day, etc.), a minute later, in the meantime, meanwhile, on the following day, at length, ultimately, presently
3. **To signal _order_ or _sequence_**	first (second, etc.), finally, hence, next, then, from here on, to begin with, last of all, after, before, as soon as, in the end, gradually
4. **To signify _space_ and _place_**	above, behind, below, beyond, here, there, to the right (left), nearby, opposite, on the other side, in the background, directly ahead, along the wall, as you turn right, at the tip, across the hall, at this point, adjacent to

5. To signal an *example*	for example, to illustrate, for instance, to be specific, such as, moreover, furthermore, just as important, similarly, in the same way
6. To show *results*	as a result, hence, so accordingly, as a consequence, consequently, thus, since, therefore, for this reason, because of this
7. To signal *purpose*	to this end, for this purpose, with this in mind, for this reason, for these reasons
8. To signal *comparisons*	like, in the same (like) manner or way, similarly
9. To indicate *contrast*	but, in contrast, conversely, however, still, nevertheless, nonetheless, yet, and yet, on the other hand, of course, on the contrary, or, in spite of this, actually, a year ago, now, notwithstanding, for all that, strangely enough, ironically
10. To signal *alternatives*, *exceptions*, and *objections*	although, though, while, despite, to be sure, it is true, true, I grant, granted, I admit, admittedly, doubtless, I concede, regardless
11. To *dispute*	it isn't true that, people are wrong who say that, deny that, be that as it may, by the same token, no doubt, we often hear it said, many people claim, many people suppose, it used to be thought, in any case
12. To *intensify*	above all, first and foremost, importantly, again, to be sure, indeed, in fact, as a matter of fact, as I have said, as has been noted
13. To *summarize* or *repeat*	in summary, to sum up, to repeat, briefly, in short, finally, on the whole, therefore, as I have said, in conclusion, as you can see

Additionally, **pronouns** act as connectives when they are used to refer to a noun in the preceding sentences. Repetition of key words and phrases and the use of **synonyms** which echo important words both serve to establish connections with previous sentences.

Retrieved 8/18/2015 from: http://www.mdc.edu/Kendall/collegeprep/documents2 /TRANSITIONAL%20WORDS%20AND%20PHRASESrevised815.pdf

Figure 2.1: Transition words and phrases.

Have a Plan—ABBC and A, Triple B, C

The plan works for paragraphs and essays that are answers to questions or petition prompts. The difference is that, for the integrated response essay (IRE), each step has a complete ABBC paragraph or page of such paragraphs, and there are, minimally, three B points of evidence. The IRE is essentially an expanded, elaborated CR—applying the A, Triple B, C plan with information integrated from multiple sources to more deeply address a prompt. Instructional steps, lessons, and examples for the CR and IRE are included in this text.

Nancy worked collaboratively with an eleventh-grade ELA teacher at the high school who was struggling with getting students to write down what they could fluently discuss. The students were reading *The Odyssey*; in discussions, they talked about the themes, characters, and settings, but when it came to writing a constructed response to the question prompt, they were stuck. Their answers were minimal—weak versions of their comments in class discussions. A typical example is as follows:

Question prompt: *Athena's meeting with Telemachus changes things for him. How does it change things, and how does he show this?*

Typical answers varied, but none answered it thoroughly or thoughtfully.

Answer 1: *He grew up and acted like a man.*

Answer 2: *Telemachus gets his eyes opened by Athena, and he takes things serious now.*

Answer 3: *Things changed for Telemachus after he met with Athena. She tells him the truth about what is happening.*

When the teacher and Nancy reviewed these answers, they realized how sparse and abbreviated they were. The next day, they put a plan into action; they went beyond explaining ABBC in an isolated way, attaching the steps to the request of the question prompt students had been given. They passed back the previous day's prompt on Telemachus and reread it.

Question prompt: Athena's meeting with Telemachus changes things for him. How does it change things, and how does he show this?

At the board, Nancy had written:

Announce

Build and Back up

Build and Back up

Connect back and Conclude

Announce: After Athena meets with Telemachus, there are noticeable changes in his understanding of their circumstances as well as what he must do.

Build and Back up: He is made aware of the reality of the suitors' intent for his mother and how they are dangerous to her, himself, and their kingdom since they want to take control.

Build and Back up: Athena teaches him to be responsible and assertive; he begins to take control of the kingdom himself.

Connect back and Conclude: These are the ways that Telemachus changes from his meeting with Athena.

As Nancy worked quietly at the board to compose this draft of an answer during the discussion, she noticed students already making revisions on their returned papers. She shared her draft with them, identifying them as collaborative authors of it and herself as merely the scribe. At that point, a student said, "We did know it, but we really didn't show it." This is when Nancy began her mantra of "Good that you *know* it, now go ahead and *show* it" in a connected, clear, and complete constructed response. She also lets students know that they are always allowed to add additional B sentences beyond the minimum and that any B in a constructed response can have more than a single sentence to explain it. Nancy emphasizes that writers initially need to intensely focus on the A step—to begin in a way that builds readers' curiosity, draws them in, and allows them to anticipate what will follow.

Nancy describes how when working collaboratively with a 15:1 classroom (fifteen special needs students and one teacher) of eleventh- and twelfth-grade students, she was reminded of how much can be learned from the students, including students you never expected would reverse the roles.

The SMART Board in the classroom had the ABBC format listed on it. As Nancy explained what each letter stood for, she wrote in the explanation. When she came to the end, she noticed that Ricky was once again not taking the notes that other students were writing down. Instead, he had started sketching a house. Frustrated, Nancy approached him and commented, "You were supposed to be taking notes. This is what will help you complete the writing portion successfully on the upcoming state exams." Ricky looked at her very seriously and said, "I *was* taking notes." With a bit of restraint, Nancy asked him to explain how his sketching was note-taking. He reminded her that she'd told the class previously not to be afraid to use visuals as part of note-taking—visuals that would help to remind them of an idea or information.

He was correct; now, Nancy asked for his explanation of the rough sketch and how it was connected to that suggestion.

Ricky explained that the top of the house is the **A**, **A**ttic, where we **A**nnounce to all what is happening. He then explained the connection to the next floor (that is, just below the attic), "On the next floor, **B**, you **B**uild it up with evidence." At this point, the teacher and Nancy looked at each other, knowing Ricky was onto something. Nancy had Ricky continue, only this time, she asked him to share with the whole class how a house visual could be a reminder of ABBC. He grinned widely and continued to explain—no, he taught the class.

"The next floor is also a **B**, to **B**uild it up with more evidence, and like you said, it can have as many **B** floors as it needs." At this point, Nancy sat down in her seat as he went on, ready to learn herself. Ricky continued with a purpose for the basement. "The house would have a **C**, Cellar, which holds it up. It's where you **C**onclude and **C**onnect back to the rest of the house." The class actually applauded him. Eleventh and twelfth graders applauding a fellow student for teaching—this was awesome! But Ricky still had to suggest one more feature. He added, "It would need a garage and car." When asked why, Nancy was impressed with his creative thinking. "It would be to remind us to use **Transition Words** that you are always going on about. The car transports to the next sentence or transitions to it," Ricky shared, smiling ear to ear. He'd definitely won the day. Nancy created figure 2.2 as a class anchor for remembering the steps of ABBC, refining and formalizing this student's idea. See figure 2.2, "House Model for ABBC."

Pause and Ponder

With colleagues, reflect on and discuss the following prompts.

1. How will you use the technique of changing the prompt into a lead to help those students who tend not to know how to begin or how to stay focused on the topic?

2. Explain how you have taught students the how and why of effective paraphrasing.

3. How well do your students (or have you observed students) use transition words? How can you use familiar texts to teach words that can be used as transitions and discuss their use in context?

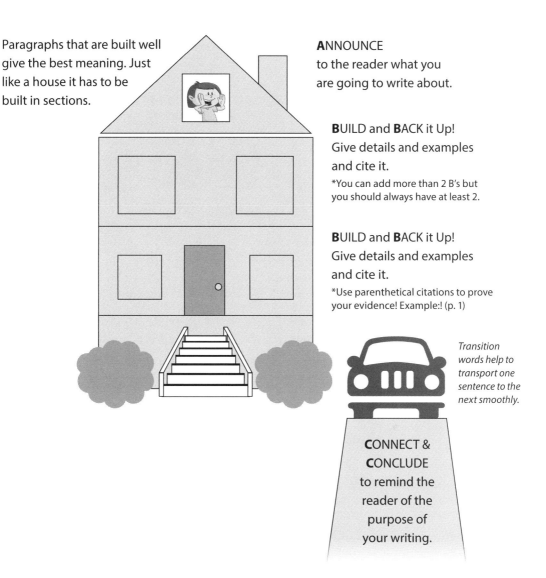

Paragraphs that are built well give the best meaning. Just like a house it has to be built in sections.

ANNOUNCE to the reader what you are going to write about.

BUILD and **B**ACK it Up! Give details and examples and cite it.

*You can add more than 2 B's but you should always have at least 2.

BUILD and **B**ACK it Up! Give details and examples and cite it.

*Use parenthetical citations to prove your evidence! Example:! (p. 1)

Transition words help to transport one sentence to the next smoothly.

CONNECT & **C**ONCLUDE to remind the reader of the purpose of your writing.

© Nancy Roberts Sept. 2015
adapted by Roberts, 2012

Figure 2.2: House model for ABBC.

CHAPTER 3

(V) Visualize the Constructed Response Paragraph

*The beautiful part of writing is that you don't have to
get it right the first time, unlike, say, a brain surgeon.*

—Robert Cormier

The ABCs of Writing a Paragraph

Before any writing begins, the student needs to carefully read, reread, and analyze the prompt to interpret exactly what is expected. It's critically important that writers take this step and then follow the restating process previously described. This ensures readers that the writer intends to respond or answer the prompt as posed. Once the writer understands what is expected, he rereads the article with the prompt's request in mind. Notes can be made on a copy of the article or on paper if the reading was in a text. See figures 3.1 and 3.2.

Introduction - reformer - worked for changes

SARAH BAGLEY: Fighter for Rights

Sarah Bagley was one of the most important women reformers in early nineteenth-century America. Born in Canada, New Hampshire, her mother and father farmed, sold land, and owned a small mill, Bagley was working in the Lowell, Massachusetts, factories as a weaver.   *textile worker herself*

After working in the mills on and off for several years, Bagley realized that employment had very little bargaining power over their employers when it came to wages and working conditions. In December 1844, Bagley and five other women formed the Lowell Female Labor Reform Association. It was organized in an attempt to improve health conditions in the mills and lobby for a ten-hour workday. Bagley became president of the association and saw it grow to nearly six hundred members.   *little bargaining power*

journalist - speaker

During this time, Bagley also wrote for and briefly edited the *Voice of Industry* newspaper, which favored the shortened workday. And, at a time when women rarely spoke at public gatherings, Bagley became famous for her speeches.

politically involved

In 1845, Bagley led the association to petition the Massachusetts legislature in demanding a ten-hour workday. The legislature agreed to have a committee hold hearings, becoming one of the first state governments in U.S. history to investigate the conditions of labor in factories. Bagley and others testified on the long hours and unhealthy working conditions in the mills. The committee, chaired by Lowell representative William Schouler, decided that the legislature did not have the legal authority to determine hours of work. Furious, the workers helped defeat Schouler in the next election.

2nd petition

Along with other labor groups in the state, Bagley and the association continued to push for shorter working hours. Ten thousand people from all over Massachusetts, including more than two thousand from Lowell, signed another petition to try once again to persuade the legislature to take action. Hearings were held a second time, and again the legislature refused to challenge the mills. Then, in 1847, Lowell textile companies voluntarily shortened their workdays by thirty minutes.

broke barriers - didn't give up

In the fall of 1846, John Allen, editor of the Voice of Industry, told Bagley that she could no longer write for the newspaper. She was told that she was too controversial and that writing was not dignified for a woman to do. Discouraged and angry, she looked for another job. The telegraph business was new, and an office had just been opened in Lowell. Bagley was hired as the first female telegrapher in the United States. Early in 1847, Bagley contracted to run a telegraph office in Springfield, Massachusetts. When she learned that she was earning three-quarters of the salary of the man she had replaced, Bagley formed an even stronger commitment to equality and women's rights.

wrote about social issues

In 1848, Bagley returned to Lowell to work in a mill again. She also traveled and wrote about health care, working conditions, prison reform, and women's rights. While visiting Philadelphia in 1849, Bagley probably met and then soon married James Durno, a doctor who used herbs for medicinal purposes to care for his patients. Bagley became an herbal doctor as well. In 1851, the couple was in Albany, New York, where their doctors' fees showed Bagley's sympathy for working people: "... to the rich, one dollar -- to the poor, gratis [free]."   *concern for fairness*

Bagley died sometime after 1883. She had lived long enough to see the ten-hour workday law enacted in Massachusetts as well as in several other states.

Lobby means to try to influence the thinking of public officials for or against proposed legislation.

Source Citation: "SARAH BAGLEY Fighter for Rights." Cobblestone 22.3 (March 2001): 35. Student Edition. Gale. Dover-Sherborn Middle School. 6 Apr. 2009
http://find.galegroup.com/itx/start.do?prodId=STOM.

Retrieved 9/19/2017 from dsmswlutz.pbworks.com/w/.../SARAH%20BAGLEY%20Fighter%20for%20Rights.

activist
politically involved
broke barriers

Conclusion —
can tie to social justice

Figure 3.1: "Sarah Bagley, Fighter for Rights."

PP: Describe three ways that Sarah Bagley acted like a leader.

Prompts adapted from Sample Reading Constructed Responses, MEAP Fall 2005 Released Texts, Michigan Department of Education.

Retrieved from

https://datadeb.files.wordpress.com/2010/02/examples-of-prompts-for-reading-constructed-response.pdf.

Notes:

Social Activist for Causes

- Worked to improve wages, organized workers
- Became president of workers' association
- Testified on long hours and unhealthy conditions

Politically Active

- Worked within legal system for change
- Petitioned legislature twice about workers' needs and rights
- Efforts led to hearings, but denied relief
- Worked to defeat committee chair who voted no on petition
- Later company voluntarily shortened workers' day

Broke Barriers for Women

- Sarah was a journalist, social topics writer, telegrapher when such roles were considered undignified for women
- When she knew she wasn't paid as a telegrapher what the man she replaced had been paid, she fought for equality for women
- She didn't give up on fair treatment for women and all groups of people

reformer – person who works to make changes to improve

social justice = everyone in a society is treated fairly

Figure 3.2: Petition prompt for Sarah Bagley article.

The teacher starts with an *I do*, rereading the article to students, reading her notes aloud, and talking about her thinking related to the article and notes. Then she explains how she interprets, specifically what the petition prompt wants her to do, making a point that this prompt for a constructed response is requesting three points of evidence—three Bs for *Build up* and *Back up*. That, she reassures them, is not a problem; they could also decide to add an extra B, or they may be asked for more than two points of evidence at any time. Here, acting as a responder, she just has to identify a third example that shows how Sarah Bagley was a leader. She mentally models how she examines the content of her notes, looking for categories or patterns of behavior that relate to *leadership*—as the prompt asks her to discuss. She thinks aloud, demonstrating how she has determined categories for her three areas of evidence (that is, activist, politically involved, and someone who broke barriers), a focus for her lead (that is, reformer), and an idea to tie concepts together in the conclusion (that is, social justice). The *I do* step is repeated with multiple examples with content related to different domains of study, where two Bs are sufficient as well as one where an additional B could be added. A single teacher demonstration is seldom, if ever, enough. Additional examples across all subject areas should be modeled by the teacher. When students have mastered reading, close reading, note-taking, determining categories, and interpreting the prompt as preparation for writing a CR, the teacher returns to one of the models for this process and starts working on the ABBC steps.

A = Announce with Introduction of the Theme: Using the Prompt to Create a Frame for a Response

Teachers often refer to the first sentence of a paragraph as a topic sentence, main idea (MI), or essential idea. The topic of a text, however, is different from its main idea. The topic is usually a word or phrase that represents the major theme of the message; the main idea is stated or implied in a sentence or across sentences. Identifying the theme of the overall text helps the writer conceptualize and organize for writing a successful constructed response for any prompt.

Direct instruction, teacher modeling, and supported practice are essential before asking any and all students to grasp these distinctions. In demonstration lessons, teachers use an authentic example to work through this step (that is, doing a think aloud / write aloud) and provide visuals of the process as well as anchor chart reminders (Gipe, 2014).

Since the opening sentence in a text isn't dependably the MI or, necessarily, an essential sentence, we will call it a lead—a sentence intended to pull the reader in to whisper, "Tell me more." The lead *announces* what will be coming with a bit of mystery and a *tease*. Nancy has heard teachers suggest some version of the following: "Just tell me what you will be writing about in the paragraph—the big picture without all the details." When Nancy worked with students on this step, they were often hesitant, afraid that they'd be wrong. She would continuously assure them that it wasn't a matter of being wrong but more about getting started and being clear without giving away the details of content that would follow. This is where she connected examples of real-world leads that announce with a *tease* of what was to come. Newspaper articles are great at this with headers and lead sentences. See figure 3.3.

Readers whisper, "Tell me more."

Header: Why Irma is so strong and other questions about hurricanes

By Associated Press

September 8, 2017

Announce Lead: A powerful Hurricane Irma is threatening millions of people. It is in the Caribbean and Florida. Here are answers to questions about Irma and hurricanes …

Retrieved from https://www.tweentribune.com/article/tween56/why-irma-so-strong -and-other-questions-about-hurricanes/.

Header: What should you do with your used eclipse glasses?

By Jason Daley, Smithsonian.com

August 24, 2017

Announce Lead: Millions of people ogled the skies using eclipse viewers. They avidly watched as the moon blotted out the sun. But now all that celestial majesty has passed. So, what should you do with your eclipse glasses?

Retrieved from https://www.smithsonianmag.com/smart-news/what-should-you -do-your-used-eclipse-glasses-180964584/.

Header: At least 20 kids dead after quake collapses Mexican school

By Joe Tacopino, Kids Post (New York Post)

September 19, 2017

Announce Lead: At least 20 children died in a school that collapsed during the devastating earthquake in Mexico, authorities said Tuesday night.

Retrieved from http://nypost.com/2017/09/20/at-least-20-kids-dead-after-quake -collapses-mexican-school/.

Figure 3.3: Newspaper headers and leads that announce with a *tease*.

The teacher initiates a conversation about each header and *announce* lead. She leads a discussion on how each grabs readers' attention and *teases*, making the reader curious and interested in reading more.

Teacher: When you listen to the morning announcements, what are they about?

Student 1: They're usually about what is going on for the day. Sometimes to tell us who won the football game. Stuff like that.

Teacher: OK, so they don't get into a lot of detail, but instead give you the general idea of something you need to know, events that already happened, or what's coming up on the schedule? You want to know more. It's a *teaser* because you're thinking, *Tell me more about that game—who played, exciting plays, and more.*

Student 1: Yes, I guess so. The announcement gets you thinking about it, but then you think, *What about this? What about that?*

Teacher: Newspaper articles are good examples of writers competing for your attention with a *tease* that pulls your eyes to an article. You read the headline (the header) and want to know more, so you read the opening lines (the lead), and you get hooked if it's a topic that interests you. The writer has your attention. You are thinking, *Tell me more.* Look at this first header and lead sentence about hurricane Irma. What catches your attention? Why?

Student 2: The header is about why Hurricane Irma was so strong. You want to know what makes the difference because some are just tropical storms.

Student 3: The lead paragraph says there will be answers to questions—probably ones that people asked—about Irma and hurricanes in general. I want to know more right now, so I'd read this article.

Teacher: Yes, that's a good example. You've got it! The writer grabbed you, hooked you in. Now, let's look at the other headers and leads.

Following discussion on more examples the teacher does a think aloud / write aloud (TA/WA) to compose a lead for her constructed response for "Sarah Bagley, Fighter for Rights"—one she expects will have readers whispering, "Tell me more."

Title: Sarah Bagley, Fighter for Rights

Announce: Sarah Bagley was a reformer who drove the fight for changes in the way workers were treated in the 19th century. She was a determined, outspoken leader who never backed down from what was right.

With students, the teacher discusses her lead and evaluates how well it accomplishes the intended goal. Multiple additional examples are completed with texts across other content areas. With this step understood, the teacher takes students to the first *Build up* and *Back up* with evidence.

B = Build Up and Back Up: Persuade with Cited Information to Support Thinking

As Nancy continued to assess how responsive students were to the first part of this new ABBC plan for writing CRs, she thought about what they needed to be successful in the next step—*Build up*, backing up with evidence. She reviewed students' prior writing samples, examining sentences that were expected to build up (that is, with reasons) the premise stated in the lead. This review was insightful. She found that too often the specifics, information, or details offered by writers as evidence were from their own thinking—their background knowledge—rather than sourced in the text read. Students didn't appear to realize the need or the process of returning to the text read to *close* read (for example, reread selected parts) for points of evidence offered by the author that could be used in their CR and sourced to the author of the text read.

Lower-level texts, especially expository ones, are more direct in presenting key ideas and details. As texts become more complex, information may be more abundant as well as reflective of different points of view (Serravallo, 2015), making evaluation of text content especially important. Notes taken as preparation for writing help writers categorize and organize information. Nancy also shares with students that they need to be aware that expository writing can have both facts and opinions—even opinions that are presented as facts. Often there are direct or implied elements of persuasion in the writing. Such bias or personal views must be differentiated from facts; critical reading to evaluate text validity is a skill included across most scope-and-sequence curricular charts (Cole, 2009), and it is essential.

Students who misunderstand the task of writing a CR connected to a text often think they already have to *know* the answer, versus building it with evidence that backs it up right in the text. Their next question was almost always the same. If not expressed, the blank expression on a student's face said volumes.

Student 1: Now that I have a lead and have announced, what do I do next?

Teacher: Now you need to *Build up* (B) your paragraph with information that will support your announcement; it gives the reader evidence for the premise or theme that you stated in the lead. You need to show readers what you learned from the text and give important details that support the premise stated in your announcement or introduction.

Student: OK, but how should I write it?

Teacher: Use what you read and reread in the text; use your notes that list details you've gathered. Remember to restructure information *in your words*. Then, cite all claims or statements of information found in the text as you have been taught and asked to do (that is, the format used at the school or district). This aligns with a particular format for citations (for example, Turabian, MLA, Chicago, APA), which would include various arrangements of author, year, page, line, and more.

Student: How many details do I have to give?

Teacher: Always give a minimum of two in a CR, but what you really need to pay attention to is how many details you are asked to give in the prompt, or add extra if you feel that's necessary to make your point or more than two areas of evidence are offered in the text. But remember, this is expected to be a CR paragraph, not a longer extended response, like an essay.

Student: So, I could have more than two *Build up* points of evidence. This is starting to make sense.

At this point, students are beginning to feel more in control of the situation. They realize that the grist for their CR is within the text read; they don't need to invent an answer or craft one from prior knowledge. Now, they know how to start, and they understand how to find supporting details for the premise stated in their lead. The teacher does a think aloud / write aloud (TA/WA).

Teacher: I'm going to look over my notes to review my thinking, details I pulled from the text, and the way I organized and categorized ideas about Sarah's leadership.

Student 1: You have three categories named and ideas under each.

Teacher: Yes. I was thinking that all the information in the article could be organized into three areas that demonstrate her leadership. One is that Sarah was an activist who fought for people's rights. Another was that she used political processes to show how the system should work when people have issues in a democracy. My third category was about her; she did things that women didn't usually attempt at that time. She broke barriers that held women back. I think I will start with the activist category as evidence for leadership qualities.

Student 2: She certainly was active, leading workers to complain about long working days and unhealthy conditions. She didn't just put up with unfair treatment.

The teacher rereads her notes in the activist category aloud. She mulls them over, verbally trying out how to craft ideas into succinct sentences. She drafts her thoughts; she rereads what she's written, revises and revises again until it sounds smooth, clear, and complete in a compact way. She checks that it also has good transitions and markers to let readers know the purpose of what's coming. Then she rewrites her first *Build up*.

Build Up, Back Up #1:

First, Sarah took on the role of social activist by leading the fight for workers' rights, seeking healthier working conditions and shorter days in the textile factories where she worked. She organized six hundred workers and served as the workers' association president (Cobblestone, 2001).

The teacher checks the flow of what she has composed so far; she reads the lead and follows immediately with the first piece of evidence. Revisions can be made if it seems choppy or doesn't transition well.

B = Build Up and Back Up: Persuade with Cited Information to Support Thinking

This process is repeated for the next point, showing evidence of leadership qualities. The teacher models in a TA/WA—rereading and thinking aloud. She talks aloud about her second category.

Teacher: My next category of ideas is about how Sarah used the political system, trying to get the state government to help. The legislators weren't receptive to the workers' pleas.

Student 1: Yeah. Sarah and the other workers helped to get the chair of the committee that didn't help them defeated when he ran for reelection. That's a way to make changes.

Teacher: That's an important point. She didn't just get angry and give up. She used the political system to effect change in policies. This Build-up will tell about that act of leadership.

The teacher drafts aloud, revises aloud, revises again, and rewrites.

Build Up, Back Up #2:

Another example of leadership was her role as the association president; she twice represented workers in petitions to the Massachusetts state legislature, trying to enlist the government in their action for workers' rights. When a state committee, chaired by William Schouler, decided they wouldn't intervene, Sarah and her coworkers helped to defeat him in his next election. Eventually, the company backed down anyway and gave them a slightly shorter workday (Cobblestone, 2001).

Again, the teacher checks the flow of what she has composed so far; she reads the lead and follows immediately with the first piece of evidence and then the next. Revisions can be made if it doesn't seem smooth or transition well.

Since this prompt called for a third example of leadership, the teacher continues in the same manner. She makes note that this prompt called for three examples of leadership, so she will need a third point of evidence.

Teacher: Minimally, CRs need two *Build up*s, but this time the prompt specifically asked for three examples of leadership. I have notes on another category I recognized. Sarah broke barriers, meaning that she went where others did not go, leading the way and showing us what could be done.

Student 1: She was a journalist for a newspaper when that kind of job was considered undignified for women.

Student 2: And when she got fired, she became a telegrapher. That was a new kind of job then, so she was a pioneer. When she found out that she was being paid less than the man she'd replaced, she wanted to fight for women's rights.

Student 3: Women are still fighting for that cause today.

Student 4: Sarah also became a writer about all kinds of social issues that affect people's lives. She was always concerned about fairness in the treatment of others and showed that in her life.

Teacher: I think we've learned a lot about Sarah and fearless leadership. I need to think about how to put this into a few sentences for my third point of evidence.

The teacher rereads her notes in the broke barriers category aloud. She mulls them over, verbally trying out how to craft ideas into succinct sentences. She drafts her thoughts; she rereads what she's written and revises and revises again until it sounds smooth, clear, and complete in a compact way.

Build Up, Back Up #3:

In her life, Sarah also broke barriers that kept women back. She was a journalist and writer when that profession was considered inappropriate for women. She became the first female telegrapher in the United States and became an advocate for women's rights and equal pay (Cobblestone, 2001).

Again, systematically, the teacher checks the flow of what she has composed so far; she reads aloud the lead and follows immediately with the first piece of evidence, then, the second, and, finally, the third aspect of Sarah's leadership. Revisions can be made where it doesn't seem smooth or transition well.

C = Connecting Back and a Strong Conclusion

The teacher mentally models her thoughts on pulling the ideas together in a way that connects, concludes, and persuades in its presentation of Sarah Bagley's leadership qualities as requested in the prompt. The teacher talks aloud about her idea of *social justice* as a tie to the opening premise and connector for these areas of evidence. Sarah's behavior throughout her life showed leadership as a reformer in the pursuit of justice for people—for social justice. An effective conclusion should tie the message parts together, close the circle by relating back to the purpose stated in the lead, give a feeling of closure like the last note in a song or musical composition, and *seal the deal* (that is, author's stated purpose).

Teacher: When you leave your house, a friend, or end a phone call, you don't just hang up out of the blue. Minimally, you say, "Bye," and, generally, a bit more.

Student 1: I say, "Gotta go. I'll talk to you later."

Student 2: I say, "I need to go. Later." I mean it as "I'll see you later."

Teacher: Why do we say such things when we end a call or visit?

Student 3: It's how we let someone know we're done for now. It's the polite thing to do; you just don't hang up or walk out.

Student 4: It's kind of like the opposite of saying hello. You start with a greeting. Then you talk about what you want to talk about. When you've finished the conversation, you let them know you're done and say, "Bye," to end it.

Teacher: When writing a CR or any composition, it's the same. It's expected that we let the reader know that we are concluding and finishing our message. An effective conclusion provides the expected closure that the reader recognizes as a wrap-up.

Students often begin simply, concluding with "This is why …" or "This is how …" As they become more adept and comfortable with writing, using the ABBC process, teachers encourage them to use a bit of personal voice, particularly in the conclusion, to sound smarter and leave an impression (Cole, 2009). Proficient writing—from start to practice—doesn't come at once; it grows slowly and with lots of practice and rewrites.

Conclusion:

Throughout her life, Sarah organized efforts and led others to use democratic systems to work for changes that improve people's lives. She took jobs that had previously been closed to women, breaking barriers that denied them opportunities. Sarah's focus was fairness for everyone; she was a humble leader—a reformer—with a passion for social justice.

Again, systematically, the teacher checks the flow of what she has composed so far; she reads aloud from the lead through the conclusion. Revisions can be made wherever it isn't smooth or doesn't transition well.

CR for the Prompt Related to "Sarah Bagley, Fighter for Rights"

Sarah Bagley, Fighter for Rights

Sarah Bagley was a reformer who drove the fight for changes in the way workers were treated in the 19th century. She was a determined, outspoken leader who never backed down from what was right. First, Sarah took on the role of social activist by leading the fight for workers' rights, seeking healthier working conditions and shorter days in the textile factories where she worked. She organized six hundred workers and served as the workers' association president (Cobblestone, 2001). Another example of leadership was her role as the association president; she twice represented workers in petitions to the Massachusetts state legislature, trying to enlist the government in their action for workers' rights. When a state committee, chaired by William Schouler, decided they wouldn't intervene, Sarah and her coworkers helped to defeat him in his next election. Eventually, the company backed down anyway and gave them a slightly shorter workday (Cobblestone, 2001). In her life, Sarah also broke barriers that kept women back. She was a journalist and writer when that profession was considered inappropriate for women. She became the first female telegrapher in the United States and became an advocate for women's rights and equal pay (Cobblestone, 2001). Throughout her life, Sarah organized efforts and led others to use democratic systems to work for changes that improved people's lives. She took jobs that had previously been closed to women, breaking barriers that denied them opportunities. Sarah's focus was fairness for everyone; she was a humble leader—a reformer—with a passion for social justice.

The teacher enlists students' assistance in scoring her CR using the rubric (figure 4.2); she goes through each line item of the rubric asking students to talk to their partner and score that line. Results are discussed; students are asked to give reasons for their scores. Let students know that no CR is perfect; there is always room for improvement. Nancy was taken aback when a secondary student, who had struggled with writing throughout earlier grades, asked a simple but insightful question: "Why didn't anyone tell us this before?" This student was able to take huge strides forward using the ABBC format; she now recognized that, with this strategy and the tools given, she could be successful. Her question and its implication drive us to provide all students with effective, comprehensive writing instruction right from the start.

Reviewing, Revising, Editing, Publishing

One way to address *polishing* writing tasks (that is, reviewing, revising, editing, and publishing) is to compare them to the work of a master gardener; with writing, the writer becomes a gardener of words. The master gardener reviews his crop to determine its state of health. Some plants are removed when there is overcrowding. Or the gardener uses a bit of organic weed killer to remove pesky intruders that are a threat to a healthy garden. Likewise, the writer removes words that act in the same way. Constant dedication and attention to care are required before a bountiful crop is harvested for market; the best crop gets the best price. Similarly, writing that has been thoroughly and thoughtfully processed before final publication will receive successful evaluations from readers.

Reviewing and revising one's writing is grueling; it requires one to read it back as a reader would—to be critical. It is usually helpful to read it back aloud and to hear whether it sounds right. Is it clear? Does it flow and pull the reader along? Does it transition well and let readers know what's coming as well as give *markers* (for example, *first*, *in addition*, *also*) for a next aspect? It's difficult to see our own errors; we tend to skip over them because our eyes see what our brains expect, knowing what we intended when we wrote it. Deleting words that we worked hard to come up with can feel like letting go of a favorite item. It's just as true, if not more so, for students who are not experienced writers who are confident that better words follow when one works at refinement. Students may feel embarrassed and even hurt with feedback suggesting word removals and corrections. The effective teacher is sensitive to each writer's self-esteem; she redirects such feelings, guiding students to consider their writer self to be like an artist who adds and removes details to make a painting a masterpiece. All writers need support; they need human support in the pedagogical ways described and they also need tools that writers use (for example, dictionaries, thesauri in print or digital form). The effective teacher shows students *how* and *where* tools can help them. Writers' tools should be made available to student writers along with consistent demonstrations of their use in different situations.

Cole (2009) suggests using *the Stranger's* (p. 78) helpful hints as guidance for writers who often "write as if the reader would already know much of the information—information that they frequently omitted" (Cole, 2009, p. 78). This imagined *stranger* is a reader who is unknown to the writer, and someone who doesn't have the opportunity to question the author. These hints encompass areas that writers need to focus on as they revise, edit, and self-assess; they align with the steps of the ABBC process. The writer asks the following.

- Can this writing be understood by a reader who never heard or read the question or prompt you were given?

- Does it flow together, connecting ideas as it is read, or does it sound like disparate, unconnected ideas?

- Are the mechanics (that is, grammar, spelling) in this writing accurate (that is, spelling, indentations, punctuation, and overall appearance)?

With samples of teacher writing (that is, with needs for revision and editing) or student work (that is, work from students who have given permission for its use), the teacher and students work collaboratively to refine each composition. Such demonstrations as *I do* and *we do* are essential before the teacher can say to students, "Now, *you do*."

Students read their work aloud to themselves, asking *the Stranger's* questions. They work on revision and editing before self-assessing their work using the CR rubric (figure 4.2). Then they read their work aloud to at least one peer to get feedback for content, clarity, and mechanics. They discuss suggestions offered, make decisions on what to accept and follow, and work on revising and editing further. The teacher will assess at this point and offer additional feedback. Finally, the writing is published to be read widely. It may also be assessed by the teacher again to determine how effectively feedback provided has been applied. In the case of state assessments requiring CR writing, feedback from others is not allowed. The writer is required to be the first and only critical reader at the revising and editing phase. The published composition reflects totally independent work. For that reason, the self-assessing aspect is very essential.

ABBC as Part of the Classroom DNA

Students depend on teachers to provide them with instruction necessary for successful performance on measures that evaluate their achievement as well as make them college and career ready—and ready to live well as citizens in the world. To fulfill those expectations, teachers must have content knowledge (what content needs to be taught), pedagogical knowledge (know and be able to effectively use efficacious instructional strategies), and conditional knowledge (understanding when and where to use particular pedagogical strategies—for example, differentiated instruction) (Boyer, 1990). Becoming an effective *communicator* in all modes of communication by the time they exit K–12 (that is, at graduation) is a goal schools should have for all students. The goal requires backward curricular design of objectives that build gradually upon each other, ensuring successful forward progress that is developmentally appropriate.

One way to help in this area is for teachers to work collaboratively. A group of stakeholders, including classroom teachers, a reading specialist or literacy coach, special educators, and administrators within the district, can be formed to review what is being asked of students at each grade level. The group reviews methods and strategies that are research-tested, reading and discussing these thoroughly. They also review what their state assessments are expecting from students and the scores students have achieved. An item analysis is conducted on previous scores, examining which items were difficult for more than a few students. The prompts for these as well as weak student responses or answers are discussed to define what was lacking. The group looks for similarities across lower-scoring CRs and establishes categories of needs. Nancy and a colleague did a *gap analysis* of various NYS Regents tests that students in the district had taken the previous June. She analyzed students' understanding of content as reflected in their answers to multiple-choice questions and overall achievement with writing in response to prompts based on readings provided. It was time well spent; analyzing the various aspects with which students struggled was insightful. See figure 3.4 that reports the percent of district students that were successful with CRs on the June 2014 exams. This knowledge was essential for planning adjustments for more responsive and targeted instruction.

Nancy Roberts (September 2014)

I reviewed the six New York State exams, which our high school students took in June of 2014. This was in an effort to see where writing needs were impacting content areas as well as ELA. The findings were not surprising, but they did offer me the opportunity to look more at our curriculum and what the exams are requiring of students. This was not formal research but rather an informative inspection of what our students achieved and where writing needs are reflecting a pattern of need in the district's ELA curriculum.

Written Response 28: 57 percent of students were successful with these tasks

Part 2 Argument

Directions: Closely read each of the four texts provided on pages 12–17 and write a source-based argument on the topic that follows. You may use the margins to take notes as you read and scrap paper to plan your response. Write your argument beginning on page 1 of your essay booklet.

Topic: Should companies be allowed to track consumers' shopping or other preferences without their permission?

Your task: Carefully read each of the four texts provided. Then, using evidence from at least three of the texts, write a well-developed argument regarding companies being allowed to track consumers' shopping or other preferences without their permission. Clearly establish your claim, distinguish your claim from alternate or opposing claims, and use specific, relevant, and sufficient evidence from at least three of the texts to develop your argument. Do not simply summarize each text.

Guidelines: Be sure to

- Establish your claim regarding companies being allowed to track consumers' shopping or other preferences without their permission.

- Distinguish your claim from alternate or opposing claims.

- Use specific, relevant, and sufficient evidence from at least three of the texts to develop your argument.

- Identify each source that you reference by text number and line number(s) or graphic (for example: Text 1, line 4, or Text 2, graphic).

- Organize your ideas in a cohesive and coherent manner.

- Maintain a formal style of writing.

- Follow the conventions of standard written English.

Part 3 Text Analysis Response

Your task: Closely read the text provided on pages 19 and 20 and write a well-developed, text-based response of two to three paragraphs. In your response, identify a central idea in the text and analyze how the author's use of one writing strategy (for example, literary element or literary technique or rhetorical device) develops this central idea.

Use strong and thorough evidence from the text to support your analysis. Do not simply summarize the text. You may use the margins to take notes as you read and scrap paper to plan your response. Write your response in the spaces provided on pages 7–9 of your essay booklet.

Guidelines: Be sure to

- Identify a central idea in the text.
- Analyze how the author's use of one writing strategy (literary element or literary technique or rhetorical device) develops this central idea. Examples include characterization, conflict, denotation/connotation, metaphor, simile, irony, language use, point of view, setting, structure, symbolism, theme, tone, and so on.
- Use strong and thorough evidence from the text to support your analysis.
- Organize your ideas in a cohesive and coherent manner.
- Maintain a formal style of writing.
- Follow the conventions of standard written English.

Figure 3.4: Gap analysis, writing achievement across academic areas.

Some teachers may say, "Oh, I won't do that; that's teaching to the test." Effective teachers examine what is needed to write authentically in any genre in or out of school and teach for that. Since academic writing is needed in school and in some careers, it is appropriate to teach it. Since formal tests are a fact of life in our educational systems, teachers need to review the expectations in these measures; translating those to students is a matter of equity. Whenever any adult knows that passing a test is required—as a gatekeeper to a promotion, certification, or qualification—he takes test preparation courses or works through self-help books to prepare. It's unfair not to help K–12 students prepare for measures that hold such weight in their school life, often operating as gatekeepers in their own way. Providing students with test savviness is simply fair practice. It's a win-win situation; both teachers and students realize success, satisfaction, and recognition of their work and effort when students can meet standards and learn what's needed to be successful in and out of school.

Teacher Demonstrations (I Do) of CR Writing

Figure 3.5 shows another teacher demonstration of a CR based on a passage read aloud, using a RA/TA (read aloud / think aloud) approach. Provide multiple such teacher or student collaborative demonstrations, showing how to respond to a CR prompt one might encounter in doing homework, on a unit quiz, or as an item on a standardized text. Certainly, this process also applies when writing a response for purposes outside of school.

CR (ABBC)—as easy as ABC—based on reading of Prairie Ecology, Center for Urban Education at DePaul University (2008). Retrieved from http://teacher.depaul.edu/Documents/PrairieEcologynonfiction6thgrade.pdf.

Petition prompt: Describe the prairie as an ecosystem.

Response: A prairie is a natural ecosystem where plants and animals live together in harmony. This can be seen in the Tallgrass Prairie in the way three particular animals live there and create a balanced environment. The skipper butterfly depends on plants in this environment throughout its life. The female butterfly lays eggs on a plant; these are protected within a shell. The larva breaks from the shell, eats the leaves of the plant, and grows. Eventually, the larva (caterpillar) forms a pupa, from which a butterfly soon emerges. The one-foot-long, brown ground squirrel lives in a large community. Since it is an herbivore, it is happy to live in a prairie with lots of grass as food and camouflage for hiding from predators. The ground squirrel sometimes eats insects, helping to keep such pests at bay. At one time, herds of bison roamed this prairie, keeping everything tidy by eating weeds that would otherwise take over the grasses. In the Tallgrass Prairie, these animals live in balance with the plants; each has what it needs to survive.

This CR has an additional B to fully report key information in the passage:

A: A prairie is a natural ecosystem where plants and animals live together in harmony. This can be seen in the Tallgrass Prairie in the way three particular animals live there and create a balanced environment.

B: The skipper butterfly depends on plants in this environment throughout its life. The female butterfly lays eggs on a plant; these are protected within a shell. The larva breaks from the shell, eats the leaves of the plant, and grows. Eventually, the larva (caterpillar) forms a pupa, from which a butterfly soon emerges.

B: The one-foot-long, brown ground squirrel lives in a large community. Since it is an herbivore, it is happy to live in a prairie with lots of grass as food and camouflage for hiding from predators. The ground squirrel sometimes eats insects, helping to keep such pests at bay.

> **B:** At one time, herds of bison roamed this prairie, keeping everything tidy by eating weeds that would otherwise take over the grasses.
>
> **C:** In the Tallgrass Prairie, these animals live in balance with the plants; each has what it needs to survive.

Figure 3.5: CR based on *Prairie Ecology*.

This type of practice continues until students are prepared to complete a successful CR independently. As a middle school reading specialist / literacy coach, Sarah Kozarowicz recognizes her job is essential in addressing students' need to learn how to write well in responding to questions. By this level, that skill is frequently requested of them across academic classes and in formal assessments. Students are expected to clearly and fully express what they know and have learned as a result of reading, instruction, discussion, research, and other information-gathering means. They are also expected to cite the sources that support claims and information they have appropriately paraphrased.

Having the right tools for such writing tasks leads students to success. Having a process that is flexible for writing across the curriculum is advantageous and efficient for writing in and out of school. Sarah has successfully used the ABBC format when collaborating with content area teachers in her school to prepare middle school writers for the writing demands in school and in life.

A change in approach began for Sarah when she provided instruction on the ABBC process and purpose as well as multiple demonstrations of both using topics associated with students' curriculum. Soon students began to participate in the writing, making it collaborative as soon as they understood *how* to plan, start, paraphrase ideas, and step-by-step cite *evidence* (that is, sources) for their knowing and thinking. Students recognized a path that could be followed from start to finish that led to success.

The samples shared here (figures 3.7–3.10) are from a health class in which Sarah collaborates with the teacher. The students read an article, "When Best Friends Break Up" (Reece, 2013), and constructed their CR as a response after learning the ABBC process; they integrated FIVES notes collected while reading the article. Students shared their work in progress with Sarah through Google Docs. As they continued with a piece of writing, Sarah was able to provide timely feedback at any time of day.

However, it's important to emphasize that before this particular lesson, before they were set off to write (that is, *you do*), these writers had had multiple demonstrations of CR writing by teachers (*I do*) and opportunities to collaborate in CR writing (*we do*) similar to the following. See figure 3.6 for Sarah's demonstration CR.

After reading the article on Hurricanes Harvey and Irma, answer the following question. Be sure to put this into paragraph format and cite the evidence you provide that supports your claim.

How were the effects of Harvey and Irma similar? Provide a minimum of two pieces of evidence that you can support from the text read.

(The following is teacher-modeled support. As she did this on the SMART Board, the teacher had students review the article and assist in citations (that is, fill in each ellipsis […].)

A) Harvey and Irma were two deadly Category 4 hurricanes that destroyed many areas of the southern United States in the summer of 2017. Both hurricanes turned people's lives upside down, and their effects will last for many years.

B) Hurricanes Harvey and Irma were historic with the wind and water damage they caused; they both forced many people to evacuate. Lives were lost. It is reported that eighty deaths are attributed to Harvey (…). Those killed across Miami, Jacksonville, and other cities as a result of Irma totaled at sixty-eight (…).

B) Hurricanes Harvey and Irma caused severe flooding where they made landfall. It appeared that floodwaters simply swallowed homes across southeast Texas (…). For a week, Harvey continued to cause damage, making roadways rivers and putting whole houses underwater (…). Flooding was also a problem in Miami, Jacksonville, and other cities when Hurricane Irma struck there (…).

B) Ace Eicher and her family had their lives turned upside down when they had to evacuate their Texas home, but they were happy to be rescued (…). Charlotte Osol and her family were among the six million Floridians who had to evacuate (…). Both families eventually returned to rebuild their lives and property.

C) The effects of Hurricanes Harvey and Irma were life-changing for many people. The road to recovery will be long, but the effects of these storms will never be forgotten!

Figure 3.6: Teacher demonstration CR.

Together, Sarah and the classroom health teacher had led students through a review of the process of using FIVES notes when writing to respond to a prompt related to assigned reading before they were asked to construct the following CR responses. Students' sense of confidence and growing competence in writing has been a true measure of success. These writers have shown increased willingness and motivation to communicate, persuade, inform, socialize, and more in writing. See figures 3.7–3.10 for student work samples based on the article on friendship read in their health class.

Name: Camryn   Date: October 20, 2017

Even the best friendships can sometimes end. What are two reasons why friendships end? What are two ways we can prevent friendships from ending?

Friendships can break up and friendships can be hard to maintain but you shouldn't let your friendships go. There are ways to keep friendships alive.

Sometimes friendships can break up because you and your friend aren't in the same classes or because you and your friend aren't interested in the same activities anymore, so you can feel distant from them. From the article "When Best Friends Break Up," John Townsend says, "Lots of relationships can be saved if you say something" (8).

Sometimes your friend's interests don't match yours, so you can feel distant. "You're not in the same classes, you rarely bump into him in the hall, and now that he's in the school play, he's spending all his time at rehearsal, while you stay busy at football practice" (4). Oliver from NYC says, "He just felt distant. We weren't as close anymore" (5).

Sometimes friendships can end, but don't let them. Friendships evolve all the time, you just need to be willing to hang on for the ride!

Name: Lily   Date: October 20, 2017

Even the best friendships can sometimes end. What are two reasons why friendships end? What are two ways we can prevent friendships from ending?

Not all friendships are meant to be. We all have friends and best friends. Which friendships are meant to be and which ones are not? Here are some tips on how to keep friendships and why some friendships just aren't meant to be.

As you get older, everyone is busy with sports and other activities. You may not get to see your friends as much anymore, but it is important that you make time to see your friends so they know that you still care about them. "Consider joining a club together, scheduling a weekly movie night, or making plans to meet up for lunch" (7).

Everyone has their own opinions on topics, and that's okay, but when it makes you and your best friend enemies, it's not okay. If you and a friend are in this situation, just give each other time to think it over. If the friendship is meant to be and you really care about each other, you will apologize and it can even make your relationship stronger. "Sometimes friends just need a little breathing room, and though it can be hard to give, it can actually strengthen a friendship" (9).

Remember, if you truly care about a friendship, you will make it through hard times and arguments together. "If my absence doesn't affect your life, my presence has no meaning."

continued →

Name: Lucas   Date: October 20, 2017

Even the best friendships can sometimes end. What are two reasons why friendships end? What are two ways we can prevent friendships from ending?

Sometimes friendships end. It might seem like the whole world is against you when it happens, but when it does happen, there's usually a reason. Friendships can survive, though, and become even stronger than before if you are willing to put in the effort.

Friendships sometimes end. They end because you might just grow apart. If you and your best bud hung out the whole school year, you may just grow apart. For example, you may go to a summer camp every year and your friend can't go. You might end up making new friends at camp and just forget about them, like in the article, it says, "It's normal for some friendships to evolve and some to dissolve" (1). One way to prevent this from happening is writing frequent letters or texts back and forth throughout the summer. This can help maintain the relationship so you can look forward to seeing them again at the end of the summer.

Another reason why friendships may end is you may get into an argument with your friend. In the article, it says, "It's normal for friends to bump heads or to need time apart" (8). For example, your friend thinks you like someone. He tells a kid at school. This person gossips about it and it somehow ends up in the ear of whoever you may or may not like. You find out and confront your friend and this turns into a heated argument. Sharp words are thrown, and feelings are hurt. Now you both think the friendship is over. A way this could be prevented is tell your friend that you don't like the person he or she accused you of liking and maybe ask if your friend can help stop the rumor before anything big happens.

Our friendships are constantly changing; however, making simple changes can create friendships that last a lifetime.

Name: Sophie   Date: October 20, 2017

Even the best friendships can sometimes end. What are two reasons why friendships end? What are two ways we can prevent friendships from ending?

Sometimes the best of friendships can come to end. Maybe you don't get to see the other person as much or you just don't have the same interests anymore. "Although friendship breakups are usually messy, experts say they don't have to be" (3).

Some friendships don't last forever and the reasons can be too many to count. One reason friendships end is that "your values, preferences, opinions, personality, or interests change" (1). One way to keep the peace between you and your friend is to give each other some time alone. Not everyone always wants to talk right away. "Sometimes friends just need a little breathing room, and though it can be hard to give, it can actually strengthen a friendship" (9). Remember, though, if your friend needs help or is feeling down, stay supportive of them. Another reason friendships end is because sometimes the two of you just don't get along anymore and just move in different directions. "As soon as two friends say adios, rumors start flying about how it ended and who 'dumped' whom" (12). Try to avoid all the gossip. It only needs to stay between you and your friend. When you're ready, tell your friend or friends how you want to move forward in your friendship. If your friendship ends, just remember to keep the peace between you and your ex-friend. "Revenge seems like a good idea, but it never is" (13).

Friendships change. It's only natural. Understanding how to deal with friendships ending and what to do in those situations can help you if you ever find yourself dealing with a fizzling friendship.

Figures 3.7–3.10: Additional work samples of a constructed response.

Writing Right from the Start

Figures 3.11 and 3.12 show a proud writer—once a reluctant writer—with his CR that has an additional B.

Starting instruction related to academic writing in elementary grades allows writers to grow developmentally, meeting appropriate performance expectations that start simply and grow in sophistication. The example for "Sarah Bagley, Fighter for Rights" is a middle school–level text with a middle school–level response. For students who have had limited writing instruction beforehand, performing at this level is a quantum leap. Teachers would have to start with much easier text and leaner CRs if students have not had sufficient direct instruction or guided practice in academic writing. Students familiar with the expectations of such academic writing are prepared to be responsive to each increasingly complex level of text and composition.

Figures 3.13–3.16 demonstrate elementary students' CR performance when provided with instruction in the ABBC format. Although they are basic in content and need refinement, they reflect understanding and purpose in fulfilling the steps of ABBC. Assuming effective instruction continues, these writers should be prepared for the reading content and writing demands when they move on to secondary levels.

10/16/2017
Prac. Fri. 20th
Read Mon 23rd

Football Rocks

by Camron

A | I am good at football. Football makes me happy. Football makes me feel emotional.

B | I feel so happy when I catch the ball. When I'm doing good I feel proud of myself. When I make a mistake I fix it.

B | My gear is comfortable. We have pads to keep us safe. When I get on the feild I smell the fresh grass. The taste of water is the best.

B | At half time we have pizza and gummies. The team mom served the food at half time.

C | Football is a good sport for me. You should try it out and see how it makes you feel.

Figure 3.11.

Figure 3.12.

My favorite hobby is reading. I like to reading whith my sister. I like to read under the tree at my house. Reading helps me learn to read.

My favorite hobby is pet care. I have a farett, a snake, and a toad. I clean up after the farett. My pets are fun to play with.

Vanessa

My favorite hobby is football. The play I did was wings half back right on 2. I'm on the left, my friend is on the right. Jake is the Quarter back. He says "bown, set, hike", I run to the ball and I grab the ball. I run to the outside, then I cut in then, I sroooooer!

Camron

My favorit hobby is gymnastics the best thing I like a bout it is you get to strech. gymnastics you get to do beckbens and back hand springs with a splits. I put on strecky clows it helpes me strech. I love this becase it kepps me bissy and this is fun and kepps me thinking.

Figures 3.13–3.16: Writing sample elementary ABBC.

Students respond well to instruction that is clear, provides a structure to follow using simple strategies, and makes connections to objectives for learning in school and the world. Figure 3.17 reflects what teachers know about a basic pedagogical principle. Meeting these needs in instructional lessons ensures effective learning and achievement.

What we found . . .

- Kids needed **structure**

- Kids needed **simple strategies**

- Kids needed to make **connections**

© 2013 Lockport City School District
Developed and Presented by: Laurie Dauphinee and Nancy Roberts

Figure 3.17.

Guided Writing Lesson for Writing a CR Lead

The detailed lesson plan provided here (figure 3.18) guides students through the same work the teacher demonstrated across several examples when taking initial notes on a text read and the prompt posed for a CR. Figures 3.19–3.22 accompany the lesson. The lesson includes an initial *you do* activity, but it is done with the support of a group and partner. Students' work scoring these CRs reinforces the elements that are required as well as their understanding of the resulting effect when they are missing.

This lesson plan is based on the passage "Teens, Texting and Driving" (Hartwell-Walker, 2016).	
Title:	**Writing a Lead**
Rationale:	Writing a strong lead, based directly on the prompt posed to the writer for a CR, guides the writer through the task. It ensures that the format is followed to complete the task as requested while ensuring that the sentences that follow the lead provide logical, text-based evidence and an appropriate conclusion that ties up and connects back to the premise or theme stated in the lead. With an effective lead, the writer has direction for building an argument.

continued ➡

Grade:	6–7
Time (# of minutes):	40–50
CCSS:	**Reading** 2, 3, 4, 6: • Explain two or more main ideas in a text and central theme. • Analyze in detail how a key individual, event, or idea is introduced, illustrated, and elaborated in a text (for example, through examples or anecdotes). • Determine the meaning of general academic and domain specific words. • Identify author's purpose.
	Writing 2, 4, 8: • Write explanatory texts in which they introduce a topic/theme. • Produce clear and coherent writing in which the development, organization, and style are appropriate to the task, purpose, and audience. • Gather information from provided sources to determine a theme or premise that will direct answering or responding to a prompt in writing.
	Speaking and Language 1–4, 6: Discussion skills
Objective: (antecedent, behavior, criterion for success)	After reviewing and rereading the article "Teens, Texting and Driving," introduced and discussed the day before, students will • work in small groups to make notes on their copy of the article as well as on their copy of the prompt to organize their response. Notes should be like those modeled (for example, with Sarah Bagley article); • share their notes; and • compose an appropriate lead for the CR prompt with a partner.
Motivating Activity: (brief activity to get attention and build interest)	• The teacher introduces the statistics image from Google images and facilitates a discussion of the content. • Students discuss their thinking and give rationale for ideas. • The teacher lets students know that they will be working with the article further to make notes as those demonstrated by the teacher when preparing to write a CR for the prompt based on "Sarah Bagley, Fighter for Rights" article.

Teacher Instruction: (teaching and modeling)	• The teacher does a RA/TA (read aloud / think aloud) with the article "Teens, Texting and Driving," emphasizing aspects that she deems important and explaining reasons for these.
	• The teacher reviews (for example, using a document camera) her note-taking for the Sarah Bagley article with students, reminding them how she reread to determine key points, underlined these, and made notes in the margins. She also determined a theme that could be used in her lead and an idea to tie information together in the conclusion.
	• The teacher reviews the notes that she wrote on her prompt sheet, categorizing information for separate Build up points of evidence.
	• She reads her lead for the Sarah Bagley article, demonstrating its theme and how her lead alludes to but doesn't give away the evidence. It gives a tease, making the reader want to know more.
Guided Practice: (students work with support of teacher or peers)	• In small groups, students reread the article on texting. They mark or highlight key information, write notes in the margin, identify a theme and an idea for their conclusion; the teacher assists as needed.
	• Students discuss their results; the teacher facilitates.
	• Students organize their notes on the article into categories, writing these on the prompt sheet; the teacher assists as needed.
	• Students discuss their results; the teacher facilitates.
Independent Practice: (students work independent of teacher)	• Explain that this independent practice will be independent of the teacher, but they will work with a partner to draft a lead for the texting article.
	• Partners use the feedback from the class discussion on their notes for evidence, categories, theme, and idea for the conclusion to write an effective lead. The partners write this on the ABBC planning chart (figure 3.22). These will be shared in class tomorrow before they start their Build up sections.

continued →

Closure: (brief summation of learning by teacher or students)	Students restate the elements needed in an effective lead—theme or premise, restatement of prompt, and a tease that entices the reader to say, "Tell me more."
Assessment: (during and after lesson)	The teacher will assess students' ability to: • Listen carefully and contribute meaningfully to class and group discussions; • Work effectively with a partner to write a draft lead for the CR; • Comprehend text, close read, and discern key ideas and a theme—as demonstrated in their notetaking and lead for a CR; • Write notes (in a group) and draft lead (with a partner).
Possible Adaptations:	1. When the teacher circulates to assist, be sure to check with ELLs and students who typically struggle on a first try with a new reading or writing skill. 2. Working with a small group of students who need more direction or support, the teacher or teaching assistant can guide students in writing notes and the draft lead.
Reflection: (completed after teaching)	

Figure 3.18: Lesson plan for writing a CR lead.

In the lesson that follows this, partners revise their lead based on the teacher's written feedback and draft two *Build up, Back up* points of evidence. They will use their notes on the article and prompt sheet to guide this. The partners write both *Build up, Back up* points of evidence on the ABBC planning chart (figure 3.22).

In a third lesson, partners revise their *Build up, Back up* points of evidence based on the teacher's written feedback and draft a conclusion. They will use their notes on the article and prompt sheet to guide this. The partners write their conclusion on the ABBC planning chart (figure 3.22).

In a final lesson, partners will revise their conclusion based on the teacher's written feedback and make a final copy of the completed CR on a separate paper. Partners will share these with two other sets of partners and get feedback. In these groups with three sets of partners, the group will score the three CRs, using the CR rubric.

Texting and Driving Statistics

These websites give detailed information on statistics related to texting and driving. Discussion of this information reinforces the very important safety message about the dangers of such behavior.

http://www.textinganddrivingsafety.com/texting-and-driving-stats

https://www.nhtsa.gov/risky-driving/distracted-driving

https://www.huffingtonpost.com/2015/06/08/dangers-of-texting-and-driving-statistics_n_7537710.html

Figure 3.19: Statistics for texting and driving.

Having been rear-ended not once but twice in the same month by teens who were texting and driving, I have a renewed interest in and alarm about the behavior. Never mind that being crashed into at 50 miles an hour turned some more of my hair gray. Never mind the inconvenience of having the car in the shop for a week at a time. Never mind the expense.

We got off easy. The teens in question only got scared, not hurt. Bumpers can be fixed. A little hair dye will cover my gray. But we and the teens may not all be so lucky next time. Sadly, there probably will be a next time unless texting and driving is made illegal and the law is rigidly enforced.

Lest you think it's no big deal, consider this: The National Highway Traffic Safety Administration reported in 2008 that driver distraction was the cause of 16 percent of all fatal crashes—5,800 people killed—and 21 percent of crashes resulting in an injury—515,000 people wounded. That was now four years ago! More teens than ever have cell phones. Chances are more teens than ever are finding it impossible to resist the urge to read or respond to texts while behind the wheel. According to the American Automobile Association, nearly 50 percent of teens admit to texting while driving. Not good. Scary.

So why, oh why, do teens persist in texting while barreling down the road at 50 miles an hour (or more), despite warnings, admonitions, and threats by parents and other concerned adults? Why don't those "X the Text" public service announcements make an impression? What's so compelling about the latest tidbit of teen connection that it is worth risking a wreck?

continued ➡

Our teens are generally good kids. But even good kids can behave thoughtlessly and badly when it comes to texting while driving. Reasons are usually some combination of these:

Denial. Teens are great at denial. They think they are invincible. They have a puffed-up sense of their own importance, competence, and invincibility. Adolescence is a time of increasing independence and an increasing belief that grownups and their opinions – even their opinions about safety – aren't relevant.

Underdeveloped impulse control. You've probably heard about it. The frontal lobe, the part of the brain that governs judgment and decision-making, doesn't fully develop until the late teens and early 20s. That's why teens are particularly likely to do crazy, risky things. They don't stop to think because the part of their brain that puts on the brakes isn't reliable. Our teens don't like it but they need us to provide the brakes until theirs are fully operational.

Myth of being a multi-tasking master. Our kids are growing up in a multi-tracked, multi-tasking world. They are often listening to music, texting their friends, and doing their homework while watching TV – all at the same time. They have an inflated idea of their competence at keeping track of everything at once. The trouble is that every task takes on equal importance. This is fine when they're watching a rerun of "South Park" while texting friends. It's not at all fine when texts are as important, or even more important, than what's going on with the traffic. In the moment a text comes in, the urge to read it is as strong as the need to keep their eyes on the road. This is an accident waiting to happen.

Overconfidence as a driver. When my kids were new drivers, I actually wished they would get into an accident serious enough to scare them but not so serious that they'd get seriously hurt. I knew parental lectures weren't getting through. Be careful what you wish for. Three of my four kids totaled cars. Fortunately, they, and the people in the other cars, walked away from those crashes unhurt. In two of the three cases, the kids were not at fault. That didn't matter. They got the message and sobered up about the reality that accidents happen even to people who are doing what they should.

I dearly wish there had been another way to get their attention. But like most teens, they were sure they would never get into an accident; that they were so good at driving that a fender-bender was the most they'd ever have to deal with.

Risk-taking high. Taking risks is an adrenalin rush. Taking risks and escaping by a hair's breadth makes the blood run and impresses friends. Teens can get enamored of risky business because squeaking by feels great! (It's the same reason people ride roller coasters even when they're scared to death.) Teens ski down trails that are beyond their skill level. They ride bikes pell-mell down rocky hills with no bike helmet. They are suckers for a dare. Unfortunately, they also sometimes like the high of speeding down the highway at 80 or playing chicken. Remember that impulse control issue? That plus the surge of adrenalin that comes from being scared is a recipe for stupid behavior.

What's a Parent to Do?

First and most important, we need to model good driving behavior. If your cell phone rings, ignore it or pull over. There are few calls that are so important that they can't be responded to a few minutes later.

If you need to make a call, pull over or ask that teen who is sitting next to you to make the call for you. A picture really is worth millions of words. Show your kids that your mind, eyes, and hands need to be on the wheel, not on the phone. You'll have no credibility at all with the kids if you demand they treat their phones differently than you do.

We need to talk to our kids. We need to talk to them often. We need to be willing to risk teen anger and take away their phones if they can't just get it that texting while driving is driving blind. They'll have lots of reasons why it's okay: "It only takes a second." "It's no different than talking to someone else in the car." "Hey. I'm great at multi-tasking." "It's the other guy who's going to cause an accident, not me." And then there's the age-old, "Everyone else is doing it."

The answers to that list are: "A second is all it takes to get in a wreck." "Talking doesn't take your eyes off the road, texting does." "Multi-tasking skills are irrelevant when you're driving a two-ton automobile at 60 miles an hour." "It's especially important to be alert when there are 'other guys' who aren't paying attention." "Everyone else doesn't concern me. You do."

Teens may not have good judgment or impulse control, but we do. If they can't show they are able to exercise self-control, they need parents to be clear that they'll provide it. There is no rule that our kids are entitled to drive our cars. If they need the car to get to a job or to school or to a game, it will be even more impressive if they have to do without it for a week or so if they break the rules. Make it clear that one infraction, just one piece of evidence that they couldn't resist the call of the cell phone, will mean the loss of both for a good long time. Then stick to it. Your teen's life may depend on it.

Figure 3.20: "Teens, Texting and Driving: Disaster in the Making" (Hartwell-Walker, 2016). https://psychcentral.com/lib/teens-exting-and-driving -disaster-in-the-making/

> **Prompt:**
>
> The article states that, despite the dire statistics and parental warnings, teens usually text while driving because of some combination of the reasons listed and explained. Identify two categories that would combine most of the reasons listed. Use these to explain possible reasons why teens engage in this behavior.

Figure 3.21: Prompt for CR related to article "Teens, Texting and Driving."

Name _____		Date _____
Tell readers what you will talk about—your theme or premise.	Give supporting reasons or evidence from the text. Cite statements or claims.	Connect back to the premise, tie points together, and conclude.
A **Announce** (write) your premise or central idea statement in a sentence. This lead should not give away your thunder; it should cause your reader to say, "Tell me more."	Always start with a central idea, theme, or premise when creating a lead. This keeps your paragraph focused on the topic. Examples: • Making choices is a central theme in … • Earthquakes have caused damage in many parts of …	Draft a lead.
B **Build Up, Back Up** Use specific examples and details from the text to support your premise. Cite your source.	Examples of possible sentence starters: First, … The text states … Another example is … Next, … In addition, … Finally, …	Draft a first point of evidence.

B **Build Up, Back Up** Use specific examples and details from the text to support your premise. Cite your source.	Same as above	Draft a second point of evidence.
C **Comments/Connections/ Conclude** Make a statement about how your examples support the premise or theme stated in the lead.	Examples of possible sentence starters: That is why … These reasons show that … This comparison explains how …	Draft a conclusion.

Source: Adapted from Roberts, 2012.

Figure 3.22: ABBC paragraphs anchor chart with suggestions.

Pause and Ponder

With colleagues, reflect on and discuss the following prompts.

1. What are the strengths and weaknesses that you have noticed in students' writing overall? In their academic writing across content areas?

2. Evaluate how well the scope and sequence of writing objectives across grades in your districts (or in districts where you have taught) appear to be thoughtful and well synchronized for achieving expected standards and outcomes in writing.

3. How could you envision using the ABBC format in your classroom? In your school? In your district?

CHAPTER 4

(E) Expand the Process to an Essay

You can always edit a bad page. You can't edit a blank page.

—Jodi Picoult

Understanding the Essay

A *constructed response* paragraph (CR) is an answer or response to a prompt that calls on the writer to demonstrate the meaning he has gathered and constructed with a text read, heard, or viewed, providing evidence from the text and experience to support points made. The paragraph reflects the elements of well-organized, focused expression of ideas and thinking. The *integrated response essay* (IRE) is distinguished from the CR by the depth and breadth of its answer or response to a prompt that calls on the writer to demonstrate broader understanding and research related to specific aspects of a topic after organizing information read, heard, or viewed. It is an elaboration of the CR structure intended to demonstrate learning, thinking, connecting, and the ability to express the knowledge one has mentally constructed across multiple sources. IRE and CR prompts may look like the following:

> **CR petition prompt:** Describe benefits and downsides of social networking websites explained in the article read.

continued ➡

IRE question prompt: How can one lessen his or her carbon footprint, becoming a better steward of the earth? What effects would be realized by such actions?

IRE petition prompt: Explain how three cost-effective alternative energy sources provide clean power with minimal negative side effects.

CR question prompt: How can Americans show support for veterans of military service and their families?

Once students have been introduced to what CR and IRE prompts look and sound like, effective writing teachers begin the modeling (*I do*) process for each step. This precedes students collaborating with the teacher (*we do*) to write content-related IREs together. Eventually, students are prepared and confident for the *you do* (independent practice)—to give it a try when they are encouraged to fly on their own, knowing that help is nearby should they falter at any point.

Step 1: Identify Key Aspects to Examine

Inquiry charts (I-Charts) are an efficient way to gather notes that relate to designated subsections of a topic (that is, aspects writers plan to examine or investigate) and ensure association of information with sources (Hoffman, 1992; Jones, 2006). The creation of the chart involves planning as well as critical thinking to determine effective and appropriate subsections. Completing the chart also involves critical and close reading to screen for information relevant to each subheading and uncover new, relevant avenues to explore.

Sometimes, students decide to add a subheading when they've discovered additional information that relates to their prompt. The first step in completing the chart is to identify the prompt and potential subtopics that address the prompt in a way that the author (that is, the writer) anticipates will justify a conclusion. This step requires abundant modeling and demonstration. A collaboratively created I-Chart and essay that follows—one related to a current unit of study—is suggested as the best way to introduce the process. The activity will cover several days. It can be completed gradually as the class is studying a unit and gathering information from multiple sources that include information on the prompt amid broader coverage of unit topics. This allows discussion on how to distinguish the relevant information for the prompt on the I-Chart and important information for other purposes. Using the IRE example in the text, *The FIVES Strategy for Reading Comprehension* (Shea & Roberts, 2016a), an I-Chart for planning would look like the one in figure 4.1.

Petition Prompt: Explain how the Civil War, despite advances in the military, reflected traditional hardships for everyone.

Topic / IRE title: New Age of Warfare with Traditional Hardships

	Build Up #1 Evidence: New Age of Warfare	Build Up #2 Evidence: Hardships for Soldiers	Build Up #3 Evidence: Civilians in the Conflict	Other Interesting Facts	Additional Build Up
What I think					
Source 1 Haskins, J. The day Fort Sumter was fired on; A photo history of the Civil War. New York, NY: Scholastic.	Newer weapons were more lethal. Troops could be moved easier and faster. Communication more effective.	10%–20% of soldiers were underage volunteers, often as drummer or bugle boy.		Civil War was first war to be covered thoroughly by the press, who risked their life to get the story.	
Source 2 Billings, J. (1987). Hardtack and coffee: The unwritten story of army life. Old Saybrook, CT: Konecky & Konecky.		More deaths due to disease than bullets. Inadequate food and supplies. Hardtack became infested with insects and hard—needed to be soaked in coffee.			

continued

Source 3 Faust, D. G. (2008). The republic of suffering. New York, NY: Reed Business Information.		Disease a major cause of deaths. Poor medical conditions.	Women had to take up the work of men called to service.	
Source 4 U.S. National Park Service. Baker, J. (n.d.). The Civil War: The civilian experience. Retrieved from www.nps.gov/resources/story.htm%eFid%3D249.	Casualties could be reported more widely and immediately with numbers and names. Conscription laws came into effect, requiring military service.	Forced into military service and leaving family.	War raged all around civilians. Civilians ravaged with diseases as well. Homes confiscated. Civilians killed in collateral damage.	Lincoln said, "We are all in this war; those who fight and those who stay at home."
Summary Summarize the information in each Build Up column for a draft of each subheading.				

Thoughts for conclusion

Politicians make the decision to go to war, but it is the citizens who fight it and pay the highest price in lives destroyed. Advantages of new equipment, ability to move troops quickly, and communicate on the battlefield didn't lessen hardships. Wars create horror for civilians caught in the path of battles.

Source: Adapted from Hoffman, 1992.

Figure 4.1: I-Chart for IRE.

The I-Chart allows the student to see where information is sparse and more research is needed, potentially new subheadings, and/or new avenues to explore in subheadings identified. Not all boxes will be filled since sources may not address each subheading. The full listing of sources has multiple benefits. Beyond making the listing of references more efficient, it is a visual connection of information to sources for rereading, checking for details, and more. Before students get started, they need to learn how to select valid and reliable sources.

Step 2: Selecting Reliable Sources

Students need to learn how to evaluate sources for usefulness to their purpose as well as for accuracy and reliability of information; they also need to consider the possibility of author bias, whether the author is an individual or organization, and whether the source is a print or digital one (Kuiper & Volman, 2008; Leu, Forzani, & Kennedy, 2013). Minimally, those characteristics must be examined very carefully. Teachers can suggest a starting place for determining that both purpose and accuracy benchmarks are met when selecting sources.

When using either print or digital sources, it's suggested that students evaluate the author's credentials for evidence of sound knowledge on the topic (Leu, Forzani, & Kennedy, 2013). Is this author a credible scientist, historian, or expert of some repute in the field? A web search for a bio of an author could be fruitful for answering such questions if the author's background and/or affiliations aren't immediately available in the print or digital source. Is the book published by a press that has a sound peer-review process supervised by a professional editor? Is the article in a professional journal where submissions are peer-reviewed before being accepted? Is it posted at a reliable website (for example, one for a trustworthy organization rather than an individual's or a commercial website)? This can be determined with a bit of Internet sleuthing as well. The teacher shows how to investigate and verify.

Searching for Relevant Information

Learning how to find relevant information that addresses the topic of the prompt among the myriad of ideas and information in a given source requires knowing how to *close* read those sections of texts identified as potentially useful. The ability to locate information in sources becomes a gatekeeping skill for students attempting to comprehend texts and express their understanding and thinking with evidence to support it (Eagleton, Guinee, & Langlais, 2003). Difficulty locating information that addresses a self-posed or assigned prompt tends to stifle curiosity for *finding out* what one wishes to know; it also depresses a student's confidence as an independent learner. Students need to know how to zero in on target information within a cache of print and digital sources; they should go to those areas to skim and scan the suspected germane material. If it appears to be pertinent, close reading should follow with accompanying note-taking on the I-Chart.

With the I-Chart topic and identified subtopics in hand, instruction on the process of initially scanning the source's TOC (table of contents), index, abstract, and/or subheadings for relevance helps students determine whether the particular source would be useful in addressing areas of the topic to be researched. The teacher models how to generate effective keywords; these are significant words in a narrowed research task used to find discrete information related to the broader topic. Keywords are searched for in the source's TOC, abstract, index, and/or subheadings (Guinee, Eagleton, & Hall, 2003; Kuiper & Volman, 2008). Most often, keywords in an index have sub-listings with page numbers; these narrow down a search further to aspects of the keyword; they also present new possibilities. It's also important to be able to think of synonyms for the keyword in mind since an author may have used that alternative word when writing about a topic; using the second choice of keyword may get the reader to the intended topic when it was assumed the source did not address it. It works similarly with digital sources.

In both print and digital searches for sources, the reader must infer whether a source will be useful from such an overview (Henry, 2006) by efficiently scanning for potentially relevant information within each (Rouet, Ross, Goumi, Macedo-Rouet, & Dinet, 2011). Instruction on these research skills is an essential component in effective ELA curriculum, particularly at upper grades. Competence as knowledge seekers enhances students' overall achievement as well as their ability to self-direct learning.

Less-skilled readers often miss potentially relevant information in print sources when they use inadequate keywords, skim and scan ineffectually, don't consider other sublistings under keywords, or fail to think of synonyms for keywords that could be checked (Rouet, 2006). Inexperienced digital searchers often *click and look*, starting with the first choice presented by the search engine. They continue down the list of results, often without carefully reading the URL for the digital source or the brief sentence related to content at the page. Their search is ineffective; typically, they fail to distinguish optimal and reliable choices.

To develop deeper analysis of search results before clicking on one, students can play *One Click*. On a SMART Board or with printed copies for all the results from a search on a topic the class is studying, the teacher initially asks questions related to the source: "Which site would you expect to be valid and reliable? Why?" After selecting and discussing rationale for a choice, click on it to examine and verify. The teacher could ask, "Which site is a commercial site? How do you know?" Then, see if students can locate the best link on the search results page for questions about content to be found there. "Which link would likely have information on the destruction of rain forests?" A similar activity could be done with several books on a topic of study. The teacher gives each small group several books. She asks questions like "Which group has a book with information on the *asteroid belt*? Which group has a book that has information on when the Hubble Space Telescope was launched?" Have the groups share how they used keywords, the TOC, and/or the index.

After selecting and discussing rationale for a website choice or page to go to in a text, have students click or go to the page. When at websites or pages in a text, the teacher engages students in selective *close* reading to find answers. At this point, sources are also examined for perceptible traces of bias or opinions stated as facts. Bias and/or rigid opinions can be found in any source, but either can often be detected in sources that have commercial interests or those representing an ideology (Fabos, 2004). Discussion follows to share answers, build understanding across sources, and make conclusions on bias.

Successful comprehension requires a synthesis of evaluated information gleaned from sources used (Jenkins, 2006). Synthesis or the integration of separate ideas is characterized by Irwin (1991) as a macrocognitive process that is considered to be a challenging part of comprehension (Keen & Zimmerman, 1997). Proficiency with deep comprehension (that is, the macro processes) evolves with effective instruction, numerous demonstrations in meaningful contexts, supported guided practice, and scaffolded independent practice. The latter is gradually faded only as the student's need diminishes.

Step 3: Recording Notes, Citing Sources

Figure 4.1 (that is, the Inquiry Chart) shows how pertinent information gathered from each source is listed across the row under the subtopic to which it relates. This makes the source for each information entry across different subtopics visually apparent. Having all the required details for the source recorded here is also handy when citing sources within the IRE as well as when listing the particulars of references at the end. This lessens confusion and backtracking when trying to match discrete details with a proper citation when writing.

As the student works with a source, he determines which subtopics the source addresses, reads those related sections of the text, and makes notes under the appropriate subtopic. If the source doesn't include information on a subtopic, the box in that column is left blank. If interesting and unexpected facts emerge—ones determined to be a potential new subtopic—notes are made in that area for the source. This note-taking for the first source moves horizontally across the I-Chart. A second source is listed in the first column, and the process is repeated until all sources have been explored. The I-Chart can be expanded horizontally (that is, to include more subtopics) or vertically (that is, to include more sources). Start with basic requirements as a foundation; as students become comfortable and successful, they typically take off to investigate more widely and report more thoroughly. Figure 4.1 demonstrates this process of recording notes.

Organizing: I-Chart Outline for Essay Writing

Once sources are exhausted, students review the completed I-Chart to determine whether they have enough information. A decision is made to move to drafting or search for more sources and information.

Before the student starts to draft the first subtopic as *Build up* evidence to his premise, he reads over the subtopic; he considers his reactions, connections, and/or inferences related to the information and records these in the *I think* box; then, he writes down key points to be made in this subtopic in a brief summary at the end of the column. The notes in this *I think* box will be used to construct a lead sentence for each subtopic (*Build up*) of evidence; the specific information in the column will follow to describe evidence for that subtopic. The process is repeated for each subtopic column. The last row of the I-Chart allows the writer to make note of any thoughts that could be used to conclude in a way that ties the pieces of evidence (that is, *Build up* points) together and connects back to the lead, allowing the reader a sense of closure and completeness—that the purpose defined was met. Once these areas are complete, the students can start a draft, keeping in mind that writing is always recursive. One can decide there's a need to return to searching for additional evidence that supports thinking or more information that clarifies details at any point.

Step 4: From I-Chart to Essay: Introduction, Subsections That Build Up, Conclusion

The writer considers the IRE prompt, the purpose intended for this essay, and how to grab readers' attention. He constructs an introductory paragraph or page built from the IRE prompt and overall awareness of the evidence discovered and recorded, just as he did when answering or responding to a CR prompt. This **Announce/**

Introduction is an ABBC paragraph or several ABBC paragraphs that set the stage for what will follow, catch readers' attention, and tease them to continue reading. The writer keeps in mind that the Announce/Introduction doesn't *give away the thunder*. It leaves the reader saying, "Tell me more" (Cole, 2009). The following examples demonstrate a possible Announce/Introduction for a CR and for an IRE. The teacher guides students' identification of similarities and differences. The CR *Announce* is for a shorter response, typically based on a single source. The IRE Announce/ Introduction sets up a longer written discussion on the topic.

Petition Prompt for CR: Erosion along its banks causes a constant movement of sediment in a river from upstream to downstream. Explain how this sediment affects a river.

Announce/Introduction Lead: The constant upstream and downstream movement of sediment in a river because of erosion has several effects. Some of these are more prominent and problematic than others.

Petition Prompt for IRE: Explain how the Civil War, despite advances in the military, reflected traditional hardships for everyone.

Announce/Introduction Lead: "Some historians claim that the Civil War initiated a modern age of warfare, particularly with technological developments. These were in the areas of communication, transportation, and weaponry. Research, reports, writings, and primary documents reveal accounts of how soldiers faced unimaginable and varied hardships awaiting battle as well as during battles. Many civilians were caught in the crosshairs, becoming collateral damage when battles were fought in their backyard. An examination of these circumstances shows that, although some aspects of warfare were new, war still had a terrible human cost" (Shea & Roberts, 2016a, p. 146).

With a lead that sets the direction—as the last sentence in each preceding lead does—the writer has a clear path to follow when writing *Build up* sections for the constructed response's ABBC or the integrated response essay's A, Triple B, C.

For the preceding CR example, the student must define and provide rationale for two (that is, *Build up* #1 and *Build up* #2 in ABBC) prominent and/or problematic effects of soil erosion and the movement of sediment. In the IRE example, the author sets out to examine what was new about warfare in Civil War time (that is, *Build up* #1 in A, Triple B, C) and how this war had a terrible human cost, as reflected in hardships inflicted on soldiers (that is, *Build up* #2) and civilians (that is, *Build up* #3). Although rereading can and should occur at any time during writing, at this particular point (that is, after drafting A and Triple B), students are led to read through their lead and the accumulation of *Build up* subsections to evaluate whether the message stays on track, presents sound reasons with clarity, and fulfills the suggested focus in the prompt. If not, they need to determine where revisions (for example, additions, deletions, rearrangement of information) would correct weaknesses.

Using the *Thoughts for conclusion* recorded on the I-Chart for the IRE or notes taken for the CR, writers compose a brief conclusion for their CR and a more elaborated one for an IRE. At first, simple conclusions are offered for CRs that closely align with the lead. Early efforts often start simply; for example, "For these reasons," "That's why," and "In conclusion" (Cole, 2009) are typical. Gradually, students become more creative in their CR conclusion, adding a bit of *punch* to persuade or surprise the reader. IRE conclusions have the same function, but these are more developed and are expected to offer a convincing and/or memorable line. Such circular closings connect back to the lead, establishing a purpose/intent, offering reasons/rationale for the position, and drawing a conclusion related to the intent, signaling readers that the writer believes he's completed his message.

CR Conclusion: For those reasons, the constant upstream and downstream movement of sediment in a river caused by erosion can have prominent and problematic effects.

IRE Conclusion: Although politicians decided to go to war, ordinary people—soldiers and civilians—paid the highest cost of that war. Some historians claim that an age of modern warfare began with the Civil War as they explain the advances in weapons, warships, troop deployment, and faster means of communication. However, these advantages didn't ease day-to-day hardships on those fighting the battles or lessen the number that died from conditions new technology didn't change. War was still horrible for those carrying out the strategies of the planners. War remained a horror for civilians living where soldiers invaded, quartered, and fought; they and their homes were in continuous danger from direct confrontations or the possibility of becoming collateral damage. Despite new methods, strategies, or advantages, war will always have terrible and enduring consequences on the humans who wage it and those who must endure it.

Step 5: Evaluating Writing Craft for CR and IRE Responses

Cole (2009) offers a simple rubric for evaluating CR responses. Before the teacher uses the rubric to evaluate individual responses, students are invited to collaboratively assess models as a class and then work in pairs to assess each other's responses. Such activities help them fully understand what's expected, exactly where their response is lacking, and what steps they need to take to improve. Figure 4.2 is a rubric for evaluating CR responses. Figure 4.3 can be used to evaluate more extended writing (for example, essay, report, research paper).

Name _____   Date _____

Topic _____

Category	Weak 1 pt	Satisfactory 3 pts	Exemplary 6 pts
Restates the prompt in the lead			
Sets a direction in the lead			
Builds up with a detail			
Builds up with a second detail			
Circular conclusion that closes and connects			
Stays on topic			
Uses conventions appropriately			
Overall total =			

Source: Adapted from Cole, 2009.

Figure 4.2: Rubric for evaluating a CR.

Name _____ Date _____

Title of Writing Piece _____

Record the date when significant evidence has been gathered to support the determination of skill level as Beginning, Developing, or Early Fluent

Skill	Beginning	Developing	Fluent
Composition			
Ideas			
• Writing is focused on a theme			
• Strong, relevant ideas are used to address the theme			
• Ideas are supported with relevant, interesting, important, or informative details			
• Message is clear to author and reader			
Organization			
• Effective opening			
• Ideas flow logically, building on each other			
• Transitions between ideas and sentences are smooth; sentences blend together			
• Effective closing			
Sentences			
• Uses simple sentences			
• Expands sentence with details and descriptors			
• Constructs appropriate compound sentences with conjunctions (for example, and, but, or)			
• Creates appropriate sentences of varied length, type, and style			
Vocabulary			
• Colorful language is used appropriately			
• Precise language is appropriately used			

• Interesting words are used appropriately			
• Effectively incorporates new words from literature and conversations			
Communication			
Purpose			
• Intention directs the writing			
• Writer can explain his intention			
• Uses writing for multiple purposes			
• Appropriately matches purpose to genre for writing			
• Effectively writes in different genres			
• Has a sense of audience; considers needs and interests of readers			
Voice			
• A personal tone comes through—a sense that the writer is speaking to a reader			
Secretary			
Mechanics			
• Tracks print while reading message back; notices missing words			
• Spelling (Beginning = semi to early phonetic; Developing = phonetic; Early Fluent = transitional to conventional)			
• Appropriate punctuation			
• Appropriate capitalization			
• Standard grammar			

continued ➡

Skill	Beginning	Developing	Fluent
Appearance			
• Print progresses from L to R, line under line (unless purposefully placed for aesthetic reasons)			
• Correct letter formation			
• Appropriate spacing between letters, words, sentences			
• Clear handwriting			
• Generally neat			
Comments:			

Source: Shea, 2015.

Figure 4.3: Writing checklist for IRE and other extended writing.

Pause and Ponder

With colleagues, reflect on and discuss the following prompts.

1. Explain how you would use the I-Chart. What variations would you suggest?

2. How have you taught students to evaluate print and digital sources? What clues have you suggested they use to distinguish credible sources in a list of URLs generated by a search engine?

3. How have you taught students to use keywords? What have you observed about students' successes and difficulties in determining keywords and being flexible with them?

CHAPTER 5

(S) Synthesize Information from Multiple Sources

The journey of a thousand miles begins with one step.

—Lao Tzu

How Is Information Across Sources Synthesized for IRE Writing?

Synthesizing notes taken during research in preparation for writing an IRE involves integrating ideas, insights, information, background experiences, and inferences collected while interacting with a variety of sources in an attempt to develop a deeper understanding of a particular issue or aspect of a broader topic.

Understanding the Plan: ABBBC—A, Triple B, C

Lamott (1994) tells the story of a time when her ten-year-old brother faced the consequences of procrastination. He was at the family's summer home at the ending days of their vacation, lamenting a report on birds that he'd had ten weeks to write but had left until the last day to start. He was at the table in the center of the cabin with pencils scattered, bird books askew, and crumpled paper around and in the wastebasket, totally overwhelmed with the enormity of the task ahead and the ticking clock. Her father, a writer himself, sat down next to his son, put his arm around to comfort him, and calmly advised, "Bird by bird, buddy. Just take it bird by bird" (p. 19). The A, Triple B, C format (that is, *Announce*, three *Build up*, *Back up* points of evidence, and a *Conclusion*) suggested for the integrated response essay (IRE) helps writers get started and follow through to create a cohesive, focused report, essay, or other extended piece of writing in any subject area. Creative flourish will come—to some more easily and readily than others—only after writers understand the basic expectations of the task and genre structure. Just as with singing, the beginning is a very good place to start for developing strong writers.

The goal of the A, Triple B, C format is to make "the processes of choosing a form, selecting ideas, generating illustrations and sentences, as transparent as possible to the students" (Hoyt, 2002, p. 244). Writing the constructed response (CR) is as simple as ABC when writers follow the structure described in chapter 3; they effectively and efficiently meet expectations and realize success. Similarly, the format for a more involved integrated response essay (IRE)—one that synthesizes information from multiple sources—is expanded from the basic CR, but it still remains as simple as ABC. It is built on a paragraph (or page) for A, one for each of three Bs (that is, *Build up*, *Back up* points of evidence), and one for the conclusion, resulting in a composition of, minimally, five paragraphs. Certainly, there can be more than three *Build up*, *Back up* points of evidence as well as multiple paragraphs or a page for each step. The teacher separately models the parts of the A, Triple B, C construction, completing a model IRE based on an I-Chart of information gathered; this is done over several lessons, just as gradually as the demonstrated CR construction in chapter 3. For each step, the teacher models the intersection of her thinking and writing, using a talk aloud / write aloud (TA/WA). Figure 5.1 can be used as an anchor chart, reminding students of the process for writing an IRE, where each paragraph within follows the ABBC format for construction. Figure 5.2 explains the steps of A, Triple B, C; it can be used as an anchor chart or a handout for each student's writing folder. Figure 5.3 provides a visual for the IRE construction, associating each step in the construction with the house concept discussed in chapter 2. Figure 5.4 provides an initial planning worksheet for writing an integrated response essay; writers identify a theme, subheadings for points of evidence, and thoughts for a conclusion that connects back to the theme or thesis. These are used with the I-Chart form in chapter 4 to remind writers of the structure to follow as they apply information, thinking, and conclusions in notes already recorded.

From Constructed Response to Integrated Response Essay (IRE)

An IRE is actually a larger constructed response that integrates information across multiple sources used to investigate the topic of the essay. The IRE is also as simple as ABC, but it has an additional B to support the premise more thoroughly. The whole IRE becomes ABBBC. An easier way to say it and remember it when thinking of IRE construction is A, Triple B, C with each paragraph following the ABBC paragraph format. It looks like this. Of course, if writers have another significant supporting category of details, they most certainly can add it to the essay with an additional B.

A—Announce with an introduction paragraph that follows the ABBC format and includes a transition leading the reader to the first category of supporting details.

B—Build up. The writer elaborates and expands on the first category of supporting details for the premise stated in the introduction in an ABBC paragraph. Cite multiple sources of information. A transition effectively draws the reader to the next category of details.

B—Build up. The writer elaborates and expands on the second category of supporting details for the premise stated in the introduction in an ABBC paragraph. Cite multiple sources of information. A transition effectively draws the reader to the third category of details.

B—Build up. The writer elaborates and expands on the third category of supporting details for the premise stated in the introduction in an ABBC paragraph. Cite multiple sources of information. A transition effectively draws the reader to the conclusion.

C—Connect back to Conclude with a Convincing statement—the three Cs. The author writes a concluding paragraph that connects back to the premise stated in the introduction and closes with a strong, convincing statement.

Source: Shea & Roberts, 2016a.

Figure 5.1: From constructed response to integrated response essay (IRE).

A, Triple B, C—as simple as ABC	
Keep it clear and show what you know.	ABBC paragraphs A) tell them what you are going to tell them; B) tell about a supporting detail; B) tell about another supporting detail; C) tell them what you told them. Remember to use good transition words to pull the reader along.
A Announce (write) your main idea or thesis statement in a sentence. Introduce the premise/topic in an ABBC paragraph.	Always write a central idea sentence first—a lead. This sentence will help keep your paragraph focused on the topic. Example: Making choices is a central theme in … or Earthquakes have caused damage in many parts of …
Triple B Build it up. Use specific examples and details to support your main idea. B B Build up three categories of support with three ABBC paragraphs.	Examples of sentence starters for Triple B with transition words and phrases 1. One example is … 2. Researchers have concluded … 3. According to multiple sources … 4. Another reason … 5. First, … 6. Then, … 7. Next, … 8. Lastly, …
C Comments/Connections/Conclude Make a statement about how your examples support your main idea. Conclude with a strong, convincing ABBC paragraph that connects to the introduction's premise.	Examples of sentence starters for C 1. It can be concluded that … 2. This shows that … 3. The totality of this information supports … 4. These examples demonstrate … 5. The evidence described appears …

Source: Shea & Roberts, 2016a.

Figure 5.2: Anchor chart for A, Triple B, C.

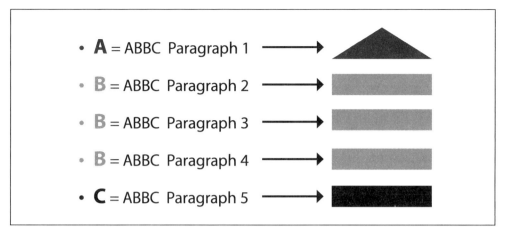

© *Roberts, 2017*

Figure 5.3: From one paragraph to multiple paragraphs for IRE.

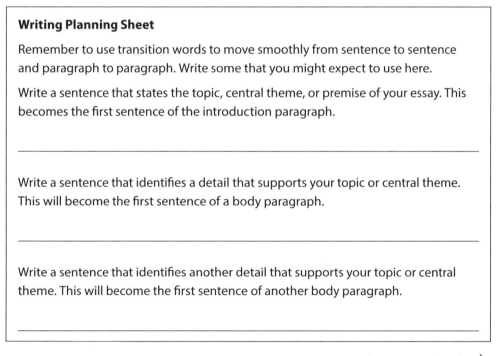

Writing Planning Sheet

Remember to use transition words to move smoothly from sentence to sentence and paragraph to paragraph. Write some that you might expect to use here.

Write a sentence that states the topic, central theme, or premise of your essay. This becomes the first sentence of the introduction paragraph.

_____

Write a sentence that identifies a detail that supports your topic or central theme. This will become the first sentence of a body paragraph.

_____

Write a sentence that identifies another detail that supports your topic or central theme. This will become the first sentence of another body paragraph.

_____

continued ➡

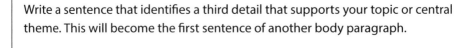

Write a sentence that identifies a third detail that supports your topic or central theme. This will become the first sentence of another body paragraph.

_____

Write a closing sentence that sums up the main point you wish to make about the topic or central theme. This becomes the first sentence of your conclusion paragraph.

_____

Source: Adapted from Gunning, 2010, p. 537.

Figure 5.4: Writing planning sheet.

Teaching in Steps: Model, Practice, Try

Getting ready to write an integrated response essay (IRE) requires analysis of the information collected and categorization into subtopics of evidence as previously stated. Consideration of one's audience, purpose, theme, rationale that supports ideas, and expectations of the genre structure to be used (Gunning, 2010) are also factors at this point. Raphael, Englert, & Kirschner (1989) noted growth in students' academic writing when instruction on text structures was paired with writing expository text. A similar strategy is RAFT. Lent (2012) credits Nancy Vandeventer (1979) with the original design of RAFT, created for use in the Montana Writing Project. Working with RAFT, writers plan their approach to the writing task, determining the *role* they will take as the author (for example, reporter, eyewitness, character), their *audience* of readers, the genre (that is, *format*) for their writing (for example, essay, news article, interview, diary), and the *topic* of the piece. Using this strategy, students become *information transformers* (Gunning, 2010, p. 534). They transform information they've synthesized into a new composition—typically in a different genre, expressing their interpretations rather than merely replicating information in paraphrased words. See figure 5.5 for a brief outline of RAFT possibilities as well as where the A, Triple B, C steps fit in the process.

Role (of writer)	Audience (readers)	Format (genre)	Topic/Theme
Newspaper reporter	Readers in the Northern states	Journalistic style— newspaper article or documentary	Civil War: New Technologies, Same Hardships of War

Figure 5.5: RAFT example.

Preparing Writers for a RAFT Assignment—Integrating the A, Triple B, C Format

The teacher explains that writers think about the point of view and stance a writer in the **role** they are assuming would have related to the **topic or theme** they intend to write about. Writers also consider the **audience**'s (that is, readers') purpose for reading the piece of writing—what they expect or hope to learn. The teacher reminds writers that using the A, Triple B, C steps with any **format** (that is, genre) will result in a well-organized, coherent, and focused composition.

Just as with the constructed response (CR), the teacher models each step of A, Triple B, C over several days; the model efficiently relates to a topic of study or issue of interest and relevance. In this way, time spent teaching the strategy is also a review of curricular content. The teacher presents her I-Chart, used to gather information on her intended topic, theme, or premise. For the model described in this chapter, the title for the demonstration IRE is "Hurricanes: Origins, Impact, and Hurricane Protection." The teacher used an I-Chart form like the one presented in chapter 4 to collect information from six sources on subheadings she identified as well as interesting details that might be used; this note-taking—as well as *how* to use the table of contents (TOC) and index provided in the texts—was modeled as each text source was shared. With websites, the teacher initially discussed how to evaluate choices offered as a result of using keywords in a search engine. The teacher reminds students that additional notes can be gathered even after draft writing begins if the writer finds that he's lacking some evidence or wishes to add another *Build up* point. In addition, FIVES notes taken during extended or previous reading on the topic can be transferred to the I-Chart with their source (Shea & Roberts, 2016a). Writing is always recursive rather than linear; writers continually go back and forth between gathering information, drafting, revising, and editing as a composition is constructed and refined. See figure 5.6 for a planning sheet on hurricanes and figure 5.7, the IRE that the teacher drafted collaboratively with students from the I-Chart constructed for it. Each ellipsis stands for a place where more writing would be done.

Writing Planning Sheet for IRE

Remember to use transition words to move smoothly from sentence to sentence and paragraph to paragraph. Write some that you might expect to use here.

Ideas come from the I-Chart. Writers can also refer to FIVES notes from extended or prior reading—along with their source—when planning (Shea & Roberts, 2016a).

Write notes for a paragraph that states the topic, thesis, theme, or premise of your essay. This becomes the introduction paragraph.

　　Most violent of storms, can take years to repair damaged property and lives

Write a heading for a paragraph that identifies a detail that supports your topic or central theme. This will be part of the first sentence of a body paragraph.

　　How they form, characteristics

Write a heading for a paragraph that identifies another detail that supports your topic or central theme. This will be part of the first sentence of another body paragraph.

　　Damage caused

Write a heading for a paragraph that identifies a third detail that supports your topic or central theme. This will be part of the first sentence of another body paragraph.

　　Protecting lives and property, what to do

Write notes for a closing paragraph that sums up the main point you wish to make about the topic or central theme. These ideas will be included in your conclusion paragraph.

Mother Nature is unpredictable, need to understand science of weather and create sustainable environment.

Source: Adapted from Gunning, 2010, p. 537.

Figure 5.6: Writing planning sheet for "Hurricanes: Origins, Impact, and Hurricane Protection."

Petition Prompt: Describe hurricanes as an extreme weather condition that impacts lives and economies

Topic/IRE Title: Hurricanes: Origins, Impact, and Hurricane Protection

(Note: Each ellipsis indicates where more details from the I-Chart would be added to the essay.)

Hurricanes: Origins, Impact, and Hurricane Protection

Hurricanes, considered to be the most violent storms that occur on Earth (NASA, 2017), form and increase their power when the ingredients for a perfect storm come together. The rise in ocean levels and water temperature is believed to have affected the number and power of hurricanes in recent seasons. When strong hurricanes hit, the impact to humans, environments, and economic stability of regions can take years to repair; lives rebuilt are not always lives restored when losses include loved ones. We have learned and continue to learn ways to protect against this extreme weather; the challenge is to heed what is known.

Origin of Hurricanes

Hurricanes in the Atlantic start off the coast of Africa, near the equator. Warm, moist air masses rise; in their place, cooler air fills in, creating low atmospheric pressure near the water's surface. The cooler air warms and the process is repeated. A cyclone of clouds, rain, and strong winds begins to spin in the area of low air pressure (NASA, 2017). A system of clouds and wind grows and spins faster, forming an eye. The eye can be forty miles across; the more violent the storm, the smaller the eye—as small as four miles across for one hurricane but larger for many others. The space immediately within the eye of the hurricane is a calm zone (Lyons, 1997). Violent cyclones develop in warmer regions of the world in the warm, moist air over the oceans; these tropical cyclones are called hurricanes in the North Atlantic Ocean, Caribbean Sea, and Gulf of Mexico (Cerveny, 1997). Once wind is 74 mph, it's a hurricane. Some grow stronger in days; others take weeks to grow large (NASA, 2017) … Hurricanes weaken over land because they lose the source of moist, warm air that they had at sea (Lyons, 1997) … Depending on the size, strength, and length of time a hurricane lasts, damage to life and property can be minimal to extremely extensive.

Impact on Lives and Property

Winds, rain, and storm surge are all elements of hurricane fury. Violent hurricanes create damage in various ways depending on the landscape where the storm hits (NASA, 2017). The wind can ………………………….. Sudden heavy rainfall creates ……………………….. Waves whipped by strong winds build on top of the storm

continued ➔

surge dome; storm surge—the bulge of seawater drawn up by wind—crashes onto the land, causing further destruction of property, levees holding back water, and sandbag walls. This creates more flooding. Storm surge can reach twenty-five feet above normal sea level (Lyons, 1997). More populated coastlines naturally put more people in danger zones ………………….. The dangers persist, but increased early warning systems and knowledge science has acquired related to building in hurricane zones and environmental conservation can save lives when they are heeded.

Hurricane Protection

People and communities can protect themselves against the deadly fury of hurricanes in many ways. Engineers have determined safer and better building techniques and materials; many of these have been implemented (Lstiburek, 2006). Newer buildings are elevated on pier structures; the first interior levels use a masonry outer structure to protect against the ravages of extreme weather. The lower level—around the piers—is used for parking and storage. Waterproof materials that dry easily when they do get wet (for example, paper-faced gypsum board and fiberglass cavity insulation) are used routinely (Lstiburek, 2006). People have become conditioned in ways to effectively prepare with supplies for securing property (for example, shuttering windows, boarding doors) and having essential survival needs (for example, food, water, gasoline, batteries, medicine, pet food, baby needs) (Allaby, 1997; Lyons, 1997). They have been educated on where to locate themselves for safety when staying in their homes and how to respond to calls to evacuate—either to shelters or out of the area (Cerveny, 2006). More long term, people have begun to consider environmental conservation and restoration projects (for example, restore wetlands, reduce CO_2 emissions) that will protect their homes and communities (NASA, 2017; De La Rosa, 2016).

We go about our lives with a sense of security and normalcy, preparing for possibilities and hoping that the worst will never affect us, but Mother Nature doesn't discriminate or favor any country, city, community, or people. She continues to humble everyone, letting us know that she has the power to significantly impact our lives and livelihood in a matter of hours with the twists and turns of her fury. Protection from hurricanes involves an understanding of the science of their formation. It also involves respecting the effects of changes observed in climate and following current knowledge for sustainable environments that adheres to sensible building codes and natural barriers. Only then can we live in relative harmony with Mother Nature—somewhat protected from her temper tantrums.

References

Allaby, M. (1997). Hurricanes. New York, NY: Facts on File.

Cerveny, R. (2006). Freaks of the storm: The world's strangest true weather stories. New York, NY: Thunder's Mouth Press.

De La Rosa, J. (2016). Understanding climate change. Chicago, IL: World Book.

Lstiburek, J. (2006). Flood and hurricane resistant buildings. Building Science Corporation. Retrieved from https://buildingscience.com/documents/digests /bsd-111-flood-and-hurricane-resistant-buildings.

Lyons, W. (1997). The handy answer weather book. New York, NY: Visible Ink.

NASA (2017). How do hurricanes form? Retrieved from https://spaceplace.nasa.gov /hurricanes/en.

Figure 5.7: IRE—"Hurricanes: Origins, Impact, and Hurricane Protection."

When a strong foundation has been built with effective instruction and demonstrations of exactly how the task is done from start to finish, writers are more comfortable jumping in to try it themselves. Letting them know that each word put down isn't carved in stone is crucial; words and sentences can be honed until the writer is satisfied. With a well-planned scope and sequence of instruction, students will grow into success with more complex academic writing tasks that involve prescribed formats for composition. "Academic writing requires adapting a third-person point-of-view and being very explicit [with information and terminology]" (Gunning, 2010, p. 536). In an extended response (for example, IRE, report), the *Announce* step (opening statements) requires, at least, a multiple-sentence paragraph but may have multiple paragraphs or even a page as its introduction.

A= Introduction: Posing a Question to Create a Frame for Research and the Essay

The draft in figure 5.7 is constructed using information from an I-Chart previously created that has collected information across sources, thinking, and conclusions as explained in chapter 4. Each aspect of the figure 5.7 IRE was completed as teacher modeling (I do) that quickly evolves into collaborative writing (we do).

The Announce step, where an introduction is created, is critically important. This is where the writer grabs the reader's attention and pulls him into the composition. Many a book, article, or report is discarded after one reads the first few paragraphs.

The reader has not been enticed to continue; what was sampled did not persuade him that continuing would be time well spent. To catch and keep the reader, the writer must open with a compelling and/or highly interesting theme or premise, leaving the reader saying, "Tell me more." Effective writing teachers show writers that the introduction may take time to mull over, thinking about what to say and how to word sentences; as any section of the composition, it will likely require rewrites before it sounds like an attention grabber.

With the students, the teacher rereads her notes across the "What I think" row on the I-Chart and mentally models how she drafts and crafts her introduction. This thinking includes inferences she's made based on newly acquired and previous schema on the issue and what she wants to describe (that is, categorically) as evidence—a skill honed across their FIVES practice (Shea & Roberts, 2016a). In a TA/WA, the teacher verbally revises before she writes and then revises after writing to rearrange, delete, and change words and sentences until the introduction flows and sounds like it would catch and hold a reader's attention, luring him in to continue reading. Word choice is a skill that effective writers attend to carefully to convey their message clearly; writers use precise words as well as topic-specific ones (Shea & Roberts, 2016a). The teacher writes her introduction for the composition on hurricanes as students observe her verbalize an ongoing thinking and constructing process. As noted, students offer suggestions that are readily accepted; collaborative writing ensues.

> *Hurricanes, considered to be the most violent storms that occur on Earth (NASA, 2017), form and increase their power when the ingredients for a perfect storm come together. The rise in ocean levels and water temperature is believed to have affected the number and power of hurricanes in recent seasons. When strong hurricanes hit, the impact to humans, environments, and economic stability of regions can take years to repair; lives rebuilt are not always lives restored when losses include loved ones. We have learned and continue to learn ways to protect against this extreme weather; the challenge is to heed what is known.*

Just as with the CR, effective transitions (that is, words and phrases) are needed to pull readers along and stimulate them to predict and expect what will follow. Smooth transitions across sentences in the introduction and from the introduction to the first paragraph (that is, *Build up* #1 point of evidence) require that students effectively apply transition words and phrases for that purpose. A list of transition words and phrases for the classroom can be obtained at http://writing2.richmond.edu/writing/

wweb/trans1.html (Tabara, 2015). Teachers continuously direct students' attention to transition words and phrases in texts read; they demonstrate how to use them in think alouds / write alouds (TA/WAs) or when writing collaboratively with students; lists of transition words are prominently posted in the classroom, reminding writers of the variety of choices they have. See figure 2.1.

B = Build Up: Persuade with Cited Information to Support First Subheading

Over the next three days, the teacher models planning and composing three *Build up*, *Back up* points of evidence—one each day. She rereads the notes in the first column—the first subheading of information. Just as with the introduction, she mentally models building sentences that report the information related to the category of information, integrating and synthesizing details across sources. A modicum of inferences, elaborations, and connections can be included to emphasize points when integrating information reported in each *Build up*, *Back up* (Shea & Roberts, 2016a). In this demonstration IRE, there are areas marked with ellipses. These are places where the teacher would complete sentences with specific details from the I-Chart, modeling how to connect and integrate note fragments across sources into well-crafted sentences. Applying personal voice, teachers complete these sentence stems—or add sentences—to convey the informational support for each point of evidence. Again, if it appears that more details are needed, sources can be revisited and searched or new sources can be located. After the first *Build up* is drafted, it is read through to check for flow as well as needs for revision and edits. Then the introduction is reread and followed by a reading of the first *Build up* evidence paragraph to determine how well a reader would be led into this section from the introduction.

Origin of Hurricanes

Hurricanes in the Atlantic start off the coast of Africa, near the equator. Warm, moist air masses rise; in their place, cooler air fills in, creating low atmospheric pressure near the water's surface. The cooler air warms and the process is repeated. A cyclone of clouds, rain, and strong winds begins to spin in the area of low air pressure (NASA, 2017). A system of clouds and wind grows and spins faster forming an eye. The eye can be forty miles across; the more violent the storm, the smaller the eye—as small as four miles across for one hurricane but larger for many others. The space immediately within the eye of the hurricane is a calm zone (Lyons, 1997). Violent cyclones develop in warmer regions of the world in the warm, moist air over the oceans; these tropical cyclones are called hurricanes in the North

Atlantic Ocean, Caribbean Sea, and Gulf of Mexico (Cerveny, 1997).
Once wind is 74 mph, it's a hurricane. Some grow stronger in days; oth-
ers take weeks to grow large (NASA, 2017) … Hurricanes weaken over
land because they lose the source of moist, warm air that they had
at sea (Lyons, 1997) … Depending on the size, strength, and length of
time a hurricane lasts, damage to life and property can be minimal to
extremely extensive.

B = Build Up: Persuade with Additional Cited Information to Support Second Subheading

The process is repeated the next day to construct *Build up #2*; the teacher uses another TA/WA. The partial report (that is, introduction and *Build up #1*) is reread to check flow, cohesion, transitions, and overall clarity. Further revisions and edits are made as the writer (that is, the teacher) deems necessary. Reading the piece aloud during these rereads of drafts is highly advised. It allows the writer to hear how his overall composition sounds, making it easier to detect points of dissonance. Places where revisions and edits are needed become more obvious when one is trying to read through the sentences aloud. After verbally reviewing the information in the column for the second subheading, mulling it over, and planning how to integrate and synthesize key ideas, the teacher completes a TA/WA, composing *Build up #2*. Again, when demonstrating, the teacher completes sentence stems (that is, shown in this example) in her voice, using information from the I-Chart. If it appears that more details are needed, sources can be revisited and searched or new sources can be located. The teacher reads the completed *Build up #2* for the second subheading aloud; she revises and edits as needed. Next, the teacher rereads the draft that now includes an Introduction, *Build up #1*, and *Build up #2*. The amount of rereading increases, but that practice fosters repeated improvements in each section as well as transitions. Writers quickly realize that every reread stimulates some type of revision or edit to improve the composition.

Impact on Lives and Property

Winds, rain, and storm surge are all elements of hurricane fury. Violent
hurricanes create damage in various ways depending on the landscape
where the storm hits (NASA, 2017). The wind can ………………………. Sudden
heavy rainfall creates ……………………… Waves whipped by strong winds build
on top of the storm surge dome; storm surge—the bulge of seawater
drawn up by wind—crashes onto the land causing further destruction
of property, levees holding back water, and sandbag walls. This creates
more flooding. Storm surge can reach twenty-five feet above normal

sea level (Lyons, 1997). More populated coastlines naturally put more people in danger zones ……………….. The dangers persist, but increased early warning systems and knowledge science has acquired related to building in hurricane zones and environmental conservation can save lives when they are heeded.

B = Build Up: Persuade with Additional Cited Information to Support Third Subheading

The third *Build up* is drafted the next day; again, all is reread to evaluate progress and how well sections connect. The message should *flow* in and across sentences, reflecting the author's building and organization of thoughts gathered; it advances steadily as a smoothly moving river—not too fast or too slow—rather than choppy and filled with the debris of disparate, unconnected bits of information. The teacher emphasizes how she must reread the draft from the stance of her critical audience, foregoing all attachment to the words she's placed on the paper. She must be prepared to rearrange, to replace, and to cull. Discarding words and rewriting sentences can be difficult for writers until they experience the process as generating an improved product. After verbally reviewing the information in the column for the third subheading, mulling it over, and planning how to integrate and synthesize key ideas, the teacher completes a TA/WA, composing *Build up* #3. The teacher reads through the completed subsection to revise, rewrite, and edit and then rereads the draft that now includes an Introduction, *Build up* #1, *Build up* #2, and *Build up* #3. Any further revisions, rewrites, or edits deemed necessary are made.

Hurricane Protection

People and communities can protect themselves against the deadly fury of hurricanes in many ways. Engineers have determined safer and better building techniques and materials; many of these have been implemented (Lstiburek, 2006). Newer buildings are elevated on pier structures; the first interior levels use a masonry outer structure to protect against the ravages of extreme weather. The lower level— around the piers—is used for parking and storage. Waterproof materials that dry easily when they do get wet (for example, paper-faced gypsum board and fiberglass cavity insulation) are used routinely (Lstiburek, 2006). People have become conditioned in ways to effectively prepare with supplies for securing property (for example, shuttering windows, boarding doors) and having essential survival needs (for example, food, water, gasoline, batteries, medicine, pet food, baby needs) (Allaby, 1997; Lyons, 1997). They have been educated on where to locate themselves for safety when staying in their homes and how *to respond to calls to evacuate—either to shelters or out of the area (Cerveny, 2006). More long term, people have begun to consider environmental conservation and restoration projects (for example, restore wetlands, reduce CO_2 emissions) that will protect their homes and communities (NASA, 2017; De La Rosa, 2016).*

C = Strong Conclusion

When the teacher, as writer, rereads her essay's introduction and three *Build up* points of evidence on the next day, she ponders aloud the thoughts (that is, conclusions, reflections, comments) in her mind, reads aloud what she's written in the I-Chart for ideas that could be useful in a conclusion, and attempts to verbally integrate and synthesize these. She drafts her conclusion slowly and tentatively, cutting and rewriting to refine sentences and ideas until she feels she has a strong conclusion. The conclusion sums up, ties up points made, and redirects to the introductory theme (Shea & Roberts, 2016a). It is the final note and opportunity the writer has to weave together the points of evidence that support his premise; it should be strongly persuasive, making its connections with a punch.

We go about our lives with a sense of security and normalcy, preparing for possibilities and hoping that the worst will never affect us, but Mother Nature doesn't discriminate or favor any country, city, community, or people. She continues to humble everyone, letting us know that she has the power to significantly impact our lives and livelihood in a matter of hours with the twists and turns of her fury. Protection from hurricanes involves an understanding of the science of their formation. It also involves respecting the effects of changes observed in climate and following current knowledge for sustainable environments that adheres to sensible building codes and natural barriers. Only then can we live in relative harmony with Mother Nature—somewhat protected from her temper tantrums.

Reviewing, Revising, Editing, Publishing

With all sections completed in draft form, the teacher demonstrates a full reread—again, as her own critical audience. It's important to emphasize the concept of *draft form* to signify that the composition is worked on continuously in each engagement with the piece of writing. The effective teacher-writer lets students know that she—as an experienced writer—reads to revise and edit *multiple* times. Mistakes and typos missed are found on a second or third review. After leaving a piece and returning to it, one finds ways to reword to improve a sentence and/or paragraph.

Rereading helps the writer recognize when and where a B (*Build up* point of evidence) may need to be further explained, expanding the paragraph or essay while providing additional information, details, and evidence. Writers also note overworked words, where more topic-specific words would add clarity, where a sophisticated (for example, colorful, stronger) word would generate interest or emphasis, and places that need a word or phrase to transition or lead the reader into another idea. Citations within the B areas are checked for format and accuracy. The format (for example, MLA, Turabian, APA) used for citations depends on the school, district, or state standards, but the necessity of using one and the process for doing it appropriately begins early and is steadily emphasized. Writers are taught to respect sources as the academic property of others; they fully acknowledge their use of ideas, statements, and the words of other writers.

One reread is never enough. Our eyes see what our brains expect will be there, making each of us our own worst editor. Diligence in attention to each word and phrase and hearing the sentences are critically important for this stage, but polishing the composition doesn't stop with the writer.

Teachers remind students that asking a peer or friend to read their work for suggestions and feedback on content and mechanics is also a good idea. Professional writers have editors who review their final draft and note places where rewriting will improve the work; before books are published, the writer works with an editor to refine each part of the book, article, or report. The teacher invites students to reread the essay with her to act as her editor. Students can work in groups after the rereading to discuss revisions and edits they'd suggest. Groups would share their lists, and these would be considered; some would be applied. It's important for the writer to maintain ownership when the original wording is acceptable—when the suggested revision is cosmetic rather than necessary.

Collaboratively, the class scores the teacher's essay, using the writing checklist (figure 4.3). Such guided experiences with the checklist and discussion in the assessment process help students understand the application of its criteria to a piece of writing, making it more likely that they would use it to self-assess work before final submission.

Figure 5.8 offers a model of an IRE based on a single source. With students who struggle at first with the complexity of multiple sources, this can be a starting place for grasping the requirements of an A, Triple B, C essay for structure and content. Differentiating the starting place and pace of moving forward in complexity ensures that students have an opportunity to be successful. Being scaffolded through the essay-writing process with a single source develops essential skills for reading to learn, paraphrasing information in personal voice, organizing ideas for presenting a theme or premise based on the reading, and writing to clearly convey a message or persuade readers of a point. Struggling writers need to experience how a successful piece of writing evolves recursively; it's not produced in a straightforward manner. Once students have been successful with the essay format using one source, teachers gradually introduce additional sources, using the I-Chart for note-taking. FIVES notes, taken previously, can also be integrated (Shea & Roberts, 2016a). This instruction and demonstration develops students' competence with integrating and synthesizing information across sources—an essential school, career, and life skill.

Three Generations of Hairstons

Mark the paragraph numbers. Read the article closely. Underline; make notes.

Most people do not know any major league baseball players. It is hard enough to even find a family in America that has just one member who plays for a big-league team. There is a family, though, that has had five of its members play professional baseball, which is more than any other family in history. They are the Hairston family.

Jerry Hairston Jr. and his younger brother, Scott, have played on many baseball teams in the major leagues. Jerry has played for nine different teams, like the Baltimore Orioles and the New York Yankees. Scott played for the Oakland Athletics and another team in New York, the Mets. However, during the 2010 season, Jerry and Scott both played on the same team, the San Diego Padres. Scott was asked about how their parents felt now that they had the chance to watch both of their sons play in the same game for the same team. "They love it. They're excited to come out and watch opening day, and watching the same game on TV is going to be something different," he told The Sporting News in 2010. Scott explained that usually their parents would have to change the channel back and forth so that they could watch Scott and Jerry play on the same night. Watching TV became much easier for the Hairston family then!

Jerry Hairston Sr. is the father of Scott and Jerry Jr. He played on a few different major league baseball teams in the 1970s and 1980s. In 1983, Jerry Sr. played an important part in an exciting game. The pitcher of that game was named Milt Wilcox. He only needed one more out for a perfect game, which is when a pitcher gets every single batter out in a game. Jerry Sr. came up to bat and got the first base hit for his team. Wilcox was probably not very happy that Jerry Sr. ruined his chance at pitching a perfect game!

Jerry Hairston Sr. also had a brother play in the major leagues. Johnny Hairston is the uncle of Scott and Jerry Jr. Like Scott, Johnny played for the Chicago Cubs, but Johnny was on the team in 1969. Johnny only played for a very short time. He played in three games and got one base hit.

Johnny and Jerry Sr.'s father also played baseball! His name was Sam Hairston, and he played for the Chicago White Sox in 1951. The grandfather of Scott and Jerry Jr. was the first black man to ever play for that team after he played in the Negro leagues for many years.

That is the story of the Hairstons: a family that has had three generations of major league baseball players.

Audio available. Retrieved from: https://www.readworks.org/article/Three-Generations-of-Hairstons/04472785-c4cb-48fa-873b-66f5b01504cd#!articleTab:content/

1. After reading this article, explain three reasons that make the Hairstons special. Provide details and cite the source.

   (Mark the question to highlight what you have to do.)

2.

A Paragraph

A The Hairston family is special for many reasons. B Their family has many professional baseball players in it. B They have five baseball players. C Each of them has played for many teams. (P1)

B Paragraph

A Two of the professional ballplayers are brothers named Jerry and Scott. B Jerry played on nine different teams. B One year, they both played for the San Diego Padres. C Their family was proud. (P2)

B Paragraph

A Scott and Jerry's father was a baseball player too. B He played during the 1970s and 1980s. B Jerry Hairston Sr. is famous for stopping a perfect game in 1983. B He got the first base hit and prevented a perfect game. C He stopped Wilcox from getting a perfect pitching game. (P3)

continued

B Paragraph

A Jerry Sr. had a brother whose name was Johnny. B Johnny played for the Cubs in 1969. B He didn't play for very long, but he did play as a professional. C All these players made the Hairston family special. (P4)

C Paragraph

A There is one more player who was very special in this family. B Jerry Sr.'s father was named Sam Hairston. B Sam played for the White Sox. C Sam, the elder member of this special family, was the very first black man who played for the White Sox team after many years of playing in the Negro league. (P5)

Figure 5.8: IRE model with a single source.

Lesson on A, Triple B, C

See figure 5.9 for a sample lesson related to the IRE; it is based on writing a strong conclusion. The importance of a gradual introduction of each step of the A, Triple B, C with a lesson for each cannot be overemphasized. Students need time to process, assimilate, and be involved in such observations of modeling by an experienced writer who explains each twist and turn, each decision—the thinking, the planning, the continuous rewriting, and the final polishing in this complex process.

This lesson plan is based on the Extreme Weather Documentary, retrieved from https://www.youtube.com/watch?v=SNfdW6R5Mx4.	
Title:	**Writing a Conclusion**
Rationale:	Writing a strong conclusion that connects back to the premise or theme, ties gathered points of evidence together, and strongly persuades readers with a punch is an essential component of a successful essay. It provides readers with a satisfying sense of closure—hopefully, convinced of the premise offered and defended in the essay. This lesson, intended to reinforce the process of crafting a strong conclusion, follows days of the teacher modeling each step of the A, Triple B, C format for an integrated response essay (IRE).
Grade:	6–7
Time (# of minutes):	40–50

CCSS:	Reading 2, 3, 4, 6:
	• Explain two or more main ideas in a text and central theme.
	• Analyze in detail how a key individual, event, or idea is introduced, illustrated, and elaborated in a text (for example, through examples or anecdotes).
	• Determine the meaning of general academic and domain-specific words.
	• Identify author's purpose.
	Writing 4:
	• Produce clear and coherent writing in which the development, organization, and style are appropriate to the task, purpose, and audience.
	Speaking and Language 1–4, 6: Discussion skills.
Objective: (antecedent, behavior, criterion for success)	After viewing the documentary on extreme weather (Extreme Weather Documentary, retrieved from https://www.youtube.com /watch?v=SNfdW6R5Mx4) (note: an ad pops up in seven minutes; click Skip Ad to continue) and discussing its introduction, points of evidence, and conclusion:
	• Small groups will compose a written conclusion for the documentary.
	• Small groups will read a newspaper article on the aftermath of an extreme weather event. (The author's conclusion for this article will have been cut.)
	• Partners will draft a strong conclusion for the newspaper article.
	• Students will evaluate conclusions written, using elements for a strong conclusion.
	• Students will independently read an article and write a conclusion for it that adheres to the expected elements.

continued ➡

Motivating Activity: (brief activity to get attention and build interest)	• The teacher reviews with students what they've gathered from the first part of a documentary on extreme weather viewed the day before—about thirty-nine minutes. This involves a review of notes she recorded as they discussed the film. • Students watch the remaining ten minutes of the documentary. The teacher adds to class notes taken the day before that relate to the documentary's introduction and points of evidence presented. • Students specifically discuss their view of the effectiveness of the documentary's conclusion with rationale for their thinking. The teacher records key ideas on the board or SMART Board. • The teacher lets students know that they will be writing a conclusion for the documentary and working with news articles to compose conclusions for those.
Teacher Instruction: (teaching and modeling)	• The teacher reviews the elements of a strong, effective conclusion (for example, using the essay on hurricanes, sharing her thinking and considerations when crafting the sentences that presented her ideas). The conclusion must connect to the theme in the introduction, tie together points of evidence presented to support the theme, and be persuasive. • The teacher reviews the theme introduced at the start of the documentary and points of evidence presented. • The teacher reviews key ideas recorded on the SMART Board that students determined were made by the documentary's author/producer in the conclusion.

Guided Practice: (students work with support of teacher or peers)	• In small groups, students compose a conclusion for a documentary (for example, expand on concepts—can't stop weather; the most you can do about the weather is predict it, be prepared, and protect against it); the teacher assists as needed. • Groups share their conclusions; the class evaluates these based on elements of connection to theme, tie-together of points of evidence, and persuasion. • Groups are given a newspaper article on an extreme weather event that has the conclusion cut. Students read the article and make notes. As a group, they discuss the header, lead, and points of evidence. • Partners construct a conclusion for the newspaper article. • Partners share their conclusions; the class evaluates each based on the elements identified for success.
Independent Practice: (students work independent of teacher)	• Students are given an article (from newspaper or Internet) on an extreme weather event (current or historical). There will be a mix of articles assigned. Students read their article, take notes on the theme and points of evidence, and write a conclusion for the article assigned to them.
Closure: (brief summation of learning by teacher or students)	• Students restate the elements needed in an effective conclusion—connection to theme, tie-together of points of evidence, and persuasion.
Assessment: (during and after lesson)	The teacher will assess students' ability to: • listen carefully and contribute meaningfully to class and group discussions; • work effectively in a group to write a draft conclusion for the documentary and with a partner to write a conclusion for a newspaper article; and • work independently to read an article, take notes as directed, and draft an appropriate conclusion for the article.

continued

Possible Adaptations:	1. When the teacher circulates to assist, she should be sure to check with ELLs and students who typically struggle on a first try with a new reading or writing skill.
	2. Working with a small group of students who need more direction or support, the teacher or teaching assistant can guide students in writing notes and the draft lead.
Reflection: (completed after teaching)	

Newspaper articles that could be used in guided practice and independent practice are listed. Concluding paragraph(s) would be cut. Students would compose a conclusion for the articles selected for use.

- "No, We Can't Control Hurricanes from Space," retrieved from https://www.livescience.com/60397-we-cannot-control-hurricanes-from-space.html.

- "Climate Change Has Influenced Timing of Europe's Floods," retrieved from http://www.climatecentral.org/news/europe-floods-climate-change-21704.

- "Here's How Climate Change Could Turn U.S. Real Estate Prices Upside Down," retrieved from http://www.climatecentral.org/news/climate-change-us-real-estate-prices-21720.

- "This is British Columbia's Second-Worst Wildfire Season. It's Far from Over," retrieved from http://www.climatecentral.org/news/british-columbia-second-worst-wildfire-season-climate-21684.

Figure 5.9: Lesson plan for writing a conclusion.

Pause and Ponder

1. What would you anticipate to be the most challenging parts for students in the process of learning to write a successful IRE? Explain. How would you plan to help them meet the challenges?

2. How is writing developmentally woven into the curriculum in your school or district? How well is it being implemented consistently and across content areas? Describe improvements you would suggest. If not yet teaching, respond based on experiences in classrooms.

3. Describe how you have taught, modeled, and emphasized the need to paraphrase ideas in personal voice, rewrite to improve expression of ideas, and revisit writing repeatedly to check work for writing craftsmanship and technical accuracy (that is, grammar, spelling, word choice).

Conclusion

He said, "There are only two days in the year when nothing can be done. One is called yesterday and the other is called tomorrow, so today is the right day to love, believe, do, and, mostly, live [—and authentically teach writing]."

—Dalai Lama

Teachers beyond primary and elementary grades have often been heard to exclaim, "I can't believe how poorly these students write! They should have learned the basics by now!" Regardless of that realization, their performance expectations for students remain the same—with objectives that too many students are unprepared to meet. Writing tasks appear to be indiscriminately assigned and assessed across grades and subject areas while the skills and strategies that students need to complete them successfully are limitedly addressed with instruction, modeling, and guided practice. Classrooms that reflect *high-operational practices* that lead to successful teaching and learning include identification of students' strengths (that is, what they know and can do related to writing), instruction targeted to writers' needs, authentic purposes for writing, students' voice and participation as teachers and learners, and, importantly, a supportive community (Jackson, 2011).

Students need to learn how to use writing as a tool to demonstrate what they have learned, wonder, believe, or feel. They imagine in writing, they try to persuade others, and they entertain with stories, recount events, or compose satirical commentaries. The list is endless as purposes and genres associated with each might become mutated when writers blur the lines in creative pursuit of self-expression. Classrooms that operate with learning at the center as the fulcrum—with a belief that everyone can be successful with the right instruction in the right amount exactly when it's needed, guided practice, genuine feedback sensitively delivered, and a caring environment—reflect a *pedagogy of confidence* (Jackson, 2011).

All students in the classroom are at a personal point in their journey of writing growth for any number of reasons. A few may be very accomplished writers, seemingly self-taught, keen observers of expert writing models, or the recipient of outside influences on their growth in this skill. Many students stumble along, developing writing skills adequately but gradually, while others continue to struggle. The etiology of gaps in writing development may be personal or related to disruptions in a student's education. Inadequate curricular planning for seamless writing development or ineffective instruction in writing, despite the best intentions of teachers, could also account for students' underperformance. Effective writing teachers ask, "*If not me, then who*? Who will determine where writers are in their development, what they need right now, and how best to provide it?"

As a lyricist, Oscar Hammerstein II wrote songs to convey a message, a story, a concept, or a personal statement using the forms of music as a *sign system*—"a symbol system used to record thinking … in a communicative form" (Shea, 2011, p. 21). He tells us, "When you sing, you begin with do-re-mi." The soloist doesn't become an opera star all at once. To sing with expression and passion, he must study and understand the story told. Music scales (that is, the forms) are learned and practiced repeatedly, building stamina to reach high and prolonged notes. So, too, it is with writing.

When you write you begin with function—that is, the intention to convey a message that is personal, interactional, heuristic, regulatory, imaginative, informative, or other (Halliday, 1975)—it's an expressive language process, a sign system as well. Young children observe the behavior of significant others around them and attempt to mimic that behavior for similar functions and purposes. They make marks intending to convey a message. Iredell (1898) concluded, "Scribbling is to writing [as] babbling is to talking" (p. 235). Yes, that was in 1898; the article can be retrieved from the Library of Congress. It seems that even at that time, some recognized and accepted young children's approximations as intentional language expressions—as a sign system. The encouragement, demonstrations, and scaffolding that flow from that stance motivates children's interest in learning the forms for written expression in their orthography, progressing from the alphabet to constructing words and building sentences. We need to start at the very beginning, teaching the youngest writers to build *bird by bird* (Lamott, 1994)—that is, sentence by sentence, paragraph by paragraph as simply as ABC—building an ABBC paragraph or an A, Triple B, C essay based on *Announce*, *Build up*, and *Conclude*.

Effective writing grows when the seed is planted—when the young writer who attempts to express thinking by making his marks is encouraged to continue and is supported in his quest with instruction that responds to what he's trying to say. When that young writer comes to school, he, hopefully, meets with curriculum that is planned to developmentally introduce skills and strategies, and spiral these (that is, revisit repeatedly) for reinforcement across grades and subject areas (Bruner, 1960) with differentiated instruction that respects learners' needs, purposes, and abilities. In the successful writing classroom, writers practice skills taught and demonstrated; they're marinated with genuine feedback, sensitively delivered in a community of writers who support each other. Writers also always have ample time to write, the liberty to make choices within parameters, and ownership of their messages.

With pedagogy and conditions in place for learning to write right from the start, teachers at secondary levels will find that most students come to their classrooms prepared to meet expected standards for writing performance. Some will, however, always exceed the norm in ways that delight readers and teachers. An example of this is a letter written for a tenth-grade ELA assignment by an accomplished writer. Students in Andrew Shea's English class had read the short story "Eisenheim the Illusionist" (Millhauser, 1990) (copy available at http://www.rakahn.com/shared/llusionist.pdf) and watched the movie adaptation, *The Illusionist* (a trailer for the movie can be found at http://www.imdb.com/title/tt0443543/). Students recorded their thinking related to transforming the story to a movie on *The Illusionist* planning sheet (figure C.1) before discussing the story as well as artistic liberties taken in the film. The RAFT assignment task was introduced and explained. Students independently wrote letters as directed. See figure C.2. The writer of the exemplary letter—shown in figure C.3—allowed her work to be shared with the class as an exemplar of writing craft. This writer has a lead that catches and keeps readers' attention, evidence that supports each point made, and a conclusion that persuades. Classmates celebrated her effort and accomplishment.

Eisenheim the Illusionist becomes The Illusionist	
+ ADD	**—**
What would you add or further develop if you were to transform "Eisenheim the Illusionist" into a feature-length film?	What would you remove or not develop if you were to transform "Eisenheim the Illusionist" into a feature-length film?
Explain your alterations.	Explain your alterations.

Figure C.1: *Illusionist* planning sheet.

Role: Writer is author of "Eisenheim the Illusionist," Steven Millhauser

Audience: Director of the film, Neil Burger

Format: Letter

Topic: Changes made to the short story to make it screen-worthy

Letter-Writing Tips

- Always proofread your letter after writing it, check for sentence structure, grammar, spelling mistakes, and so on.

- Proofread your letter again (and again) after you have revised it.

- Keep the recipient in mind; write in a way that he or she can easily understand the letter.

- Don't use abbreviated dates; for example, use November 19, 2016, not 11/19/16.

- Be respectful when you write, even if you are writing a letter of complaint.

Task:

You are writing a letter to Neil Burger, the director of the movie *The Illusionist*, in the persona of Steven Millhauser, the original author of "Eisenheim the Illusionist." It is first-person point of view. You will address the changes made to the short work to make it screen-worthy. How do you think Millhauser would have responded to the insertion of the love story, the illusion of murder, the small acts of kindness demonstrated by Eisenheim, or other changes?

Write at least a one-page letter outlining your feelings. Sign it appropriately and demonstrate that you have a more than a superficial understanding of the short story and the movie.

Figure C.2: RAFT assignment task.

XXXXXXX Street

XXXXXXXXX, XX

September 21, 2017

Dear Mr. Neil Burger,

After days of curiosity and wondering how my story could have been transformed, I was finally able to watch your adaptation of my story be brought to life in a way I never thought possible. While, at first, I was hesitant at the idea of my story being transformed into a film, I quickly accepted the idea. I was ever so curious as to how my story would have to be changed to become a big-screen movie.

Now, I must admit that I was worried. I did not believe that there was a way for my story to have been created into a film without too much alteration and changing of the plot in its entirety. Yet somehow, Mr. Burger, I believe you have done it. In my opinion, your addition of characters, including a love interest for Eisenheim in Sophie and an obvious protagonist against Eisenheim in Prince Leopold, helped to extend the plot while still leaving the main idea of the story. I also enjoyed how these additional characters and occurrences added more dialogue. As well as adding depth and a plot into the storyline, dialogue adds an overall mood to a story. Your added dialogue and relationships between various people gave the film a newfound thrill, suspense, and emotion that my story did not necessarily possess entirely. I was pleased to see that, although much was altered, you did manage to keep the illusions that Eisenheim performed, especially the illusions of the people that he "brought to life"—the main topic and allure of the movie. Likewise, I found it intriguing and brilliant that you decided to begin the film with the ending scene of the story, and how you went back in time and worked your way up to that point, giving the audience something to anticipate. Lastly, but certainly not least, was your idea to incorporate a murder into everything else occurring in the story. While, at first, I found this addition unnecessary and undermining to the way you had brilliantly developed the story, the end scene made me take back my prior disappointment and had me smiling along with Uhl, as he realized what had happened. I found this clarification and the answering of many questions to be an excellent end to the story.

If you had told me when I first wrote "Eisenheim the Illusionist" that someone would be able to turn it into a phenomenal, captivating film, I would have laughed in your face. Never in my life did I imagine this piece to be turned into something as fantastic as you have made it. And for that, I both applaud and thank you. It has truly been a privilege.

     Sincerely,

     Steven Millhauser

Note: Student's original submission; teacher feedback/suggestions for revision removed.

Figure C.3: Student's exemplary unedited letter.

When teachers write themselves, they understand the necessity to write often and persistently to hone the craft. It is hard work that requires a great deal of effort and stamina—a passion for getting it right. Teachers who write, teach writing effectively; they have bravely faced competing emotions in their writing lives as a result of readers' critiques—that is, *the thrill of victory and the agony of defeat* (to quote Jim McKay on ABC's *Wide World of Sports*). Writers, like athletes, hope for the first but use the latter to learn, to identify areas for improvement, to work harder, and become better with practice. Through experience in similar states of composition production, these teachers fully understand what writers want and need, empathize with their frustrations, and know how to advise them through the brambles and tangles of the process.

Input determines output. To increase exemplary performances, schools must examine the efficiency of their curriculum planning, and classrooms must measure the efficacy of the instruction that occurs within them. Effective changes will come—however glacial in speed—from steady action based on the results of such collaborative study.

References

Anderson, L. W., Krathwohl, D. R., Airasian, P. W., Cruikshank, K. A., Mayer, R. E., Pintrich, P. R., Raths, J., & Wittrock, M. C. (2001). *A taxonomy for learning, teaching, and assessing: A revision of Bloom's Taxonomy of educational objectives* (Complete ed.). New York, NY: Longman.

Applebee, M., & Langer, J. (2006). *The state of writing instruction: What existing data tell us.* Albany, NY: Center on English Learning and Achievement.

Beck, I., McKeown, M., & Kucan, L. (2002). *Bringing words to life: Robust vocabulary instruction.* New York, NY: Guilford Press.

Bintz, W. (2011). Teaching vocabulary across the curriculum. *Middle School Journal, 42*(4), 44–53.

Boyer, E. (1990). *Scholarship reconsidered: Priorities of the professoriate.* Princeton, NJ: Carnegie Foundation for the Advancement of Teaching.

Bruner, J. (1960). *The process of education.* Cambridge, MA: Harvard University Press.

Caine, R. N., & Caine, G. (1997). *Education on the edge of possibility.* Alexandria, VA: Association for Supervision and Curriculum Development.

Calkins, L. (1994). *The art of teaching writing.* Portsmouth, NH: Heinemann.

Cambourne, B. (1999). Conditions for literacy learning: Turning learning theory into classroom instruction: A mini case study. *Reading Teacher, 54*(4), 414–429.

Christenson, T. A. (2002). *Supporting struggling writers in the elementary classroom.* Newark, DE: International Reading Association.

Clay, M. (2001). *Change over time in children's literacy development.* Portsmouth, NH: Heinemann.

Cobblestone. (2001). Sarah Bagley: Fighter for rights. *Cobblestone, 22*(3), 35. Retrieved from dsmswlutz.pbworks.com/w/.../SARAH%20BAGLEY%20 Fighter%20for%20Rights.

Cohen, V., & Cowen, J. E. (2011). *Literacy for children in an informational age: Teaching reading, writing, and thinking.* Belmont, CA: Wadsworth Cengage Learning.

Cole, A. (2006). *Right-answer writing.* Portsmouth, NH: Heinemann.

Cole, A. (2007). Writing: An unexamined gatekeeper. *Education Week, 26*(25), 31–33.

Cole, A. (2009). *Better answers: Written performance that looks good and sounds smart.* Portland, ME: Stenhouse.

Council of Chief State School Officers (CCSSO) & National Governors Association (NGA). (2010). *Common Core State Standards for English language arts & literacy in history/social studies, science and technical subjects.* Washington, DC: Common Core State Standards Initiative.

Culham, R. (2003). *Six + 1 traits of writing.* New York, NY: Scholastic.

Cunningham, A., & Stanovich, K. (2001). What reading does for the mind. *Journal of Direct Instruction, 1*(2), 137–149.

Dyson, A. (2003). *The brothers and sisters learn to write: Popular literacies in childhood and school cultures.* New York, NY: Teachers College Press.

Eagleton, M., Guinee, K., & Langlais, K. (2003). Teaching Internet literacy strategies: The hero project. *Voices from the Middle, 10*(3), 28–35.

Fabos, B. (2004). *Wrong turn on the information superhighway: Education and the commercialization of the Internet.* New York, NY: Teachers College Press.

Ferretti, R., MacArthur, C., & Dowdy, N. (2000). The effects of elaborated goal on the persuasive writing of students with learning disabilities and their normally achieving peers. *Journal of Educational Psychology, 92,* 694–702.

Fischer, D., & Frey, N. (2007). Implementing a schoolwide literacy framework: Improving achievement in an urban elementary school. *Reading Teacher, 61,* 32–45.

Fisher, D., Frey, N., & Williams, D. (2002). Seven literacy strategies that work. *Educational Leadership, 60*(3), 70–73.

Gere, A. R. (1985). *Roots in the sawdust: Writing to learn across the disciplines.* Urbana, IL: National Council of Teachers of English.

Gilbert, J., & Graham, S. (2010). Teaching writing to elementary students in grades 4–6: A national survey. *Elementary School Journal, 110,* 494–518.

Gipe, J. P. (2014). *Multiple paths to literacy: Assessment and differentiated instruction for diverse learners, K–12* (8th ed.). Upper Saddle River, NJ: Pearson Education.

Goodlad, J. (2004). *A place called school* (20th anniversary ed.). New York, NY: McGraw-Hill.

Graham, S., & Harris, K. (2005). Improving the writing performance of young struggling writers: Theoretical and programmatic research from the Center on Accelerating Student Learning. *Journal of Special Education, 39*(1), 19–33.

Graham, S., Harris, K. R., & Troia, G. A. (1998). Writing and self-regulation: Cases from the self-regulated strategy development model. In D. H. Schunk & B. J. Zimmerman (Eds.), *Self-regulated learning from teaching to self-regulative practice* (pp. 20–41). New York, NY: Guilford Press.

Graham, S., Hebert, M., & Harris, K. (2011). Throw 'em out or make 'em better? State and district high-stakes writing assessments. *Focus on Exceptional Children, 44*(1), 1–12.

Graham, S., & Perin, D. (2007). *Writing next: Effective strategies to improve writing of adolescents in middle and high school*. Washington, DC: Alliance for Excellent Education.

Guinee, K., Eagleton, M. B., & Hall, T. E. (2003). Adolescents' Internet search strategies: Drawing on familiar cognitive paradigms when accessing electronic information sources. *Journal of Educational Computing Research*, *29*, 363–374.

Gunning, T. (2010). *Creating literacy instruction for all children* (7th ed.). New York, NY: Allyn & Bacon.

Halliday, M. (1975). *Learning how to mean: Explorations in the development of language*. London, England: Edward Arnold Publishers.

Harris, K., & Graham, S. (1999). Programmatic intervention research: Illustrations from the evolution of self-regulated strategy development. *Learning Disabilities Quarterly*, *22*, 251–262.

Hartwell-Walker, M. (2016). Teens, texting and driving: disaster in the making. *Psych Central*. Retrieved from https://psychcentral.com/lib/teens-texting-and-driving-disaster-in-the-making.

Henry, I. (2006). SEARCHing for an answer: The critical role of new literacies while reading on the Internet. *Reading Teacher*, *59*, 614–627.

Hoffman, J. (1992). Critical reading/thinking across the curriculum: Using I-Charts to support learning. *Language Arts*, *69*(2), 121–127.

Hoyt, L. (2002). *Make it real: Strategies for success with informational text*. Portsmouth, NH: Heinemann.

Hudson, P., Miller, S. P., & Butler, F. (2006). Adapting and merging explicit instruction within reform based mathematics classrooms. *American Secondary Education, 35*(1), 19–32.

Iredell, H. (1898). Eleanor learns to read. *Educator*, 233–238.

Irwin, J. (1991). *Teaching reading comprehension processes* (2nd ed.). Upper Saddle River, NJ: Prentice Hall.

Jackson, Y. (2011). *The pedagogy of confidence: Inspiring high intellectual performance in urban schools*. New York, NY: Teachers College Press.

Jenkins, H. (2006). *Convergence culture: Where old and new media collide*. New York, NY: New York University Press.

Jenkins, J., Stein, M., & Wysocki, K. (1984). Vocabulary learning through reading. *AERA Journal*, *21*(4), 767–787.

Jensen, E. (2001). "Fragile brains." *Educational Leadership*, *59*(3), 32–36.

Jones, R. (2006). *Strategies for Reading Comprehension: Inquiry Chart*. Retrieved from http://www.readingquest.org/strat/ichart.html.

Keen, E., & Zimmerman, S. (1997). *Mosaic of thought* (2nd ed.). Portsmouth, NH: Heinemann.

Kindle, K. J. (2009). Vocabulary development during Read-Alouds: Primary practices. *Reading Teacher, 63*(3), 202–211.

Kipper, K. J., & Duggan, T. J. (2006). Writing to learn across the curriculum: Tools for comprehension in content area classes. *Reading Teacher, 59*(5), 462–470.

Kucer, S. (1985). The making of meaning: Reading and writing as parallel processes. *Written Communication, 2*, 317–336.

Kuiper, E., & Volman, M. (2008). The Web as a source of information for students in K–12 education. In I. Coiro, M. Knobel, C. Lankshear, & D. Leu (Eds.), *Handbook of research on new literacies* (pp. 241–246). Mahwah, NJ: Erlbaum.

Lamott, A. (1994). *Bird by bird: Some instruction on writing and life.* New York, NY: Anchor Books.

Lent, R. C. (2012). *Textbook fatigue: 21st century tools to revitalize teaching and learning.* Alexandria, VA: Association for Supervision and Curriculum Development.

Lerner, J. (1997). *Learning disabilities: Theories, diagnosis, and teaching strategies* (7th ed.). New York, NY: Houghton Mifflin Company.

Lesley, M., & Matthews, M. (2009). Place-based essay writing and content area literacy instruction for pre-service secondary teachers. *Journal of Adolescent & Adult Literacy, 52*(6), 523–533.

Leu, D. J., Forzani, E., & Kennedy, C. (2013). Providing classroom leadership in new literacies: Preparing students for their future. In S. B. Wepner, D. S. Strickland, & D. Quatroche (Eds.), *The administration and supervision of reading programs* (5th ed.) (pp. 200–213). New York, NY: Teachers College Press.

Leu, D. J., Jr., Leu, D. D., & Coiro, J. (2004). *Teaching with the Internet: New literacies for new times* (4th ed.). Norwood, MA: Christopher-Gordon.

Luria, A. R. (1998). The development of writing in the child. In M. Kohl de Oliveria & J. Valsiner (Eds.), *Literacy in human development.* Stamford, CT: Abex Publishing.

MAEP. (2005). Prompt #2 for Sarah Bagley, Fighter for Rights. MI Department of Education. Retrieved from https://datadeb.files.wordpress.com/2010/02/examples-of -prompts-for-reading-constructed-response.pdf.

Mason, L., Harris, K., & Graham, S. (2002). Every child has a story to tell: Self-regulated strategy development for story writing. *Education and Treatment of Children, 25,* 496–506.

McDermott, M. (2010). Using multimodal writing tasks in science classrooms. *Science Teacher, 77,* 32–36.

McLaughlin, M., & Allen, M. B. (2000). *Guided comprehension: A teaching model for grades 3–8.* Newark, DE: International Reading Association.

Millhauser, S. (1990). Eisenheim the illusionist. In S. Millhauser, *The Barnum Museum stories* (American Literature). New York, NY: Poseidon Press, 215–237.

Misulis, K. E. (2009). Promoting learning through content literacy instruction. *American Secondary Educator, 37*(3), 10–18.

Mooney, M. (1990). *Reading to, with, and by children*. Katonah, NY: Richard Owens.

National Assessment Governing Board. (2007). *Writing framework for the 2011 National Assessment of Educational Progress* (pre-publication ed.). Iowa City, IA: ACT.

National Commission on Writing. (2004). *A ticket to work or a ticket out: A survey of business leaders*. Washington, DC: College Board.

Newman, S. (1984). *The craft of children's writing*. Portsmouth, NH: Heinemann.

Newman, S. (2004). Introducing children to the world of writing. *Early Childhood Today, 18*(4), 34–39.

Parsons, S. A., & Ward, A. E. (2011). A case for authentic tasks in content area literacy. *Reading Teacher, 64*(4), 462–465.

Persky, H., Daane, M., & Jin, Y. (2002). *The nation's report card: Writing 2002, NCES 2003*. Washington, DC: National Center for Educational Statistics.

Phenix, J. (1990). *Teaching writing: The nuts and bolts of running a day-to-day writing program*. Markham, Ontario, Canada: Pembroke Publishers.

Phinney, M. 1988. *Reading with the troubled reader*. Portsmouth, NH: Heinemann.

Purcell-Gates, V., Duke, N., & Martineau, J. (2007). Learning to read and write genre-specific text: Roles of authentic experience and explicit teaching. *Reading Research Quarterly, 42*(1), 8–45.

Pytash, K., & Ciecierski, L. (1995). Teaching from a disciplinary literacy stance. *Voices from the Middle, 22*(3), 14–18.

Raphael, T. E., Englert, C. S., & Kirschner, B. W. (1989). Acquisition of expository writing skills. In S. I. McMachon & T. E. Raphael (Eds.), *The book club connection: Literacy learning and classroom talk* (pp. 69–88). New York, NY: Teachers College Press.

Ray, K. W. (1999). *Wondrous words: Writers and writing in the elementary classroom*. Urbana, IL: NCTE.

Reece, T. (2013). *When best friends break up*. Retrieved from http://www.scholastic.com /choices.

Rouet, J. F. (2006). *The skills of document use: From text comprehension to web-based learning*. Mahwah, NJ: Routledge.

Rouet, J. F., Ross, C., Goumi, A., Macedo-Rouet, M., & Dinet, I. (2011). The influence of surface and deep cues on primary and secondary school students' assessment of relevance in web menus. *Learning and Instruction, 21*(2), 205–219.

Rushton, S. (2001). Applying brain research to create developmentally appropriate learning environments. *Young Children, 56*(5), 76–82.

Salahu-Din, D., Persky, H., & Miller, J. (2008). *The nation's report card: Writing 2007* (NCES 2008-468). Washington, DC: National Center for Educational Statistics, Institute of Education Sciences, U. S. Department of Education.

Schickedanz, J. (1999). *Much more than the ABCs: The early stages of reading and writing.* Washington, DC: National Association for the Education of Young Children.

Scott, R. (1993). *Spelling: Sharing the secrets.* Toronto, Ontario, Canada: Gage Publishing.

Serravallo, J. (2015). *The reading strategies book: Your everything guide to developing skilled readers.* Portsmouth, NH: Heinemann.

Shaughnessy, M. (1977). *Errors and expectations: A guide for the teacher of basic writing.* New York, NY: Oxford University Press.

Shea, M. (2011). *Parallel learning of reading and writing in early childhood.* New York, NY: Routledge.

Shea, M. (2012). *Running records: Authentic instruction in early childhood education.* New York, NY: Routledge.

Shea, M. (2015). Differentiating writing instruction: Meeting the diverse needs of authors in a classroom. *Journal of Inquiry and Action in Education, 6*(2), 79–118.

Shea, M., Murray, R., & Wright, A. W. (2015). Writing in science: Expressing understanding of text through a constructed response. *Illinois Reading Journal, 43*(4), 9–19.

Shea, M., & Roberts, N. (2016a). *The FIVES strategy for reading comprehension.* West Palm Beach, FL: Learning Sciences International.

Shea, M., & Roberts, N. (2016b). FIVES: An integrated strategy for comprehension and vocabulary learning. *Journal of Inquiry and Action in Education, 8*(1), 95–108.

Smith, F. (1988). *Insult to intelligence: The bureaucratic invasion of our classrooms.* Portsmouth, NH: Heinemann.

Streitwieser, B., Light, G., & Pazos, P. (2010). Entering the community of practitioners: A science research workshop model. *Change, 42*(3), 17–23.

Tankersley, K. (2007). *Tests that teach.* Alexandria, VA: Association for Supervision and Curriculum Development.

Taraba, J. (2015). *Writers' web: Focusing/connecting ideas.* University of Richmond Writing Center. Retrieved from http://writing2.richmond.edu/writing/wweb/trans1.html.

Tierney, R., & Readence, J. (2000). *Reading strategies and practices: A compendium.* Boston, MA: Allyn & Bacon.

Tompkins, G. (2010). *Literacy for the 21st century: A balanced approach* (5th ed.). New York, NY: Allyn & Bacon.

Vacca, J., Vacca, R., Gove, M., Burkey, L., Lenhardt, L., & McKeon, C. (2009). *Reading and learning to read* (7th ed.). New York, NY: Pearson.

Vandeventer, N. (1979). A process to structure pre-writing. *Highway One: A Canadian Journal of Language, 26,* 256–259.

Zimmerman, S., & Hutchins, C. (2003). *7 Keys to comprehension: How to help your kids read it and get it!.* New York, NY: Three Rivers Press.